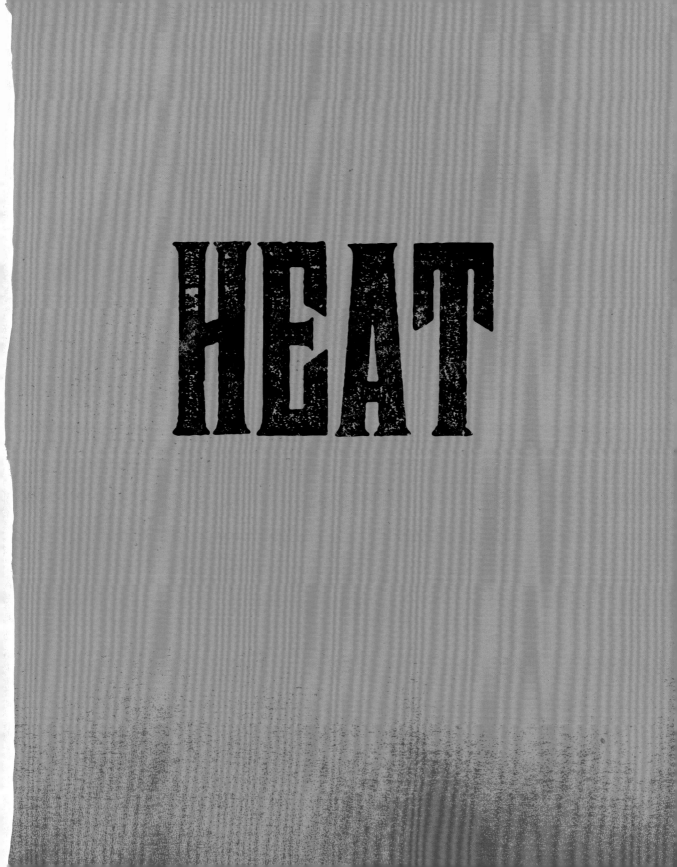

HEAT

COOKING WITH CHILLIES
the WORLD'S FAVOURITE SPICE

KAY PLUNKETT-HOGGE

Quercus

THIS BOOK IS DEDICATED TO DAD, WHO MOVED TO BANGKOK ALL THOSE YEARS AGO AND STARTED THE LOVE AFFAIR WITH HEAT. AND TO FRED, WHO KEEPS THE FLAME BURNING.

CONTENTS

INTRODUCTION

It's a fiery little fruit. And somehow, from humble origins in a small corner of Latin America, the chilli has found its way around the world and become the essential spicy ingredient in the cooking of numerous countries. So completely has the chilli been embraced, it's hard to imagine many cuisines without it.

I've been eating chillies all my life, and cooking with them since the first time I stood at a stove. Born and brought up in Thailand, it was Thai food that first gave me my chilli fix; then it was the vast range of cuisines available through the international community of sixties and seventies Bangkok, something which left me with a deep curiosity for the food of other countries. And then it was travel. I have been fortunate to live and work in four thriving multicultural cities in the course of my career: London, Los Angeles, Bangkok and New York. In each place I have been able to access and discover extraordinary cooking from around the world. This has shaped my approach to food and especially to chillies, an ingredient that is at once familiar and then again profoundly different in its many international culinary contexts.

So this is a book about cooking with chillies rather than a book about the chilli itself. For the science and history of the chilli, there are guides available that will take you into the chilli's story far more deeply than I can (though the next few pages give you a taster). But what I have tried to do is to show how to use chillies in new ways, as well as some traditional uses and recipes from around the world. All too often, one pops to the shops only to find a choice of 'red' or 'green' chillies, with no guidance on variety or relative heat. As we home cooks become more curious, we demand more – we want to know what we're buying and how to use it. So, in this book, I have used a broad range of different chillies, and flagged up substitutions wherever possible. If you can't find a variety, please don't let it put you off trying the dish. Use the chart on page 17 to find a substitution of comparable heat, and give it a go.

Or, if you're green-fingered, grow them yourself. Key to the chilli's global success is that even someone like me, Enemy of Gardens, can grow a chilli plant. There are plenty of seed specialists out there, not to mention the many chilli festivals, farms and fairs around the world where you can buy plants to grow at home.

Most importantly, while chilli is the main character in this book, my recipes are not about how much heat you can bear. Spicing is about balancing and enhancing the other tastes in a dish to bring out their best qualities. Heat for its own sake kills all other flavours, and simply packing a dish with fire is bad cooking. Furthermore, it's an insult to the chilli, a jolly little chap with far more to give. So this is not a book about blowing the back of your tongue off. Instead, it's a celebration of all the diversity the chilli has to offer.

As to my chilli choices, well, I confess that many of the recipes feature my favourites. What's a girl to do? And, while I'm admitting to that, I also make no apologies for the number of Thai recipes in the book – after all, that's where my love affair with the chilli began.

These are recipes amassed in the course of some 30 years of cooking. There are dishes I've had cooked for me by friends from all over the world, dishes I've discovered on my travels and dishes I've dreamt up in my chilli-fevered brain. As with so many meals and recipes, most come with specific stories and memories that make them special to me. At the end of it all, we can bang on about good produce (and we should), fancy utensils and gadgets, and obscure ingredients as much as we like, but, really, food is about people – the people who grow it and the people who make it; the people we share it with at our table and the stories we tell as we eat.

THE CHILLI'S JOURNEY

The very latest research, led by University of California plant scientist Paul Gepts, has proven pretty much beyond doubt that the chilli was first cultivated in central-east Mexico, most likely in the Valley of Tehuacán, some 6,500 years ago. To put this into context, the global population was a tiddling five million at the time, and in other parts of the world we were only just turning our hands to pottery. The Americas kept the chilli to themselves – quite wisely, some would say – until 1492, when one Christopher Columbus sailed the ocean blue . . .

His mission, funded by the King and Queen of Spain, was to open up a new trade route to the Indies in search of spice. For, long before oil, pepper was known as 'black gold' – exorbitantly expensive and highly desired. Though Columbus never found India in the west, he did find, on the island of Hispaniola, something with the same spicy qualities as the pepper he was seeking: a plant the local Arawak Indians called axi – the chilli. He brought it home. And thus the chilli's travels beyond the Americas began. It gave Europeans a brand new flavour profile. Along with its friends, tomato and potato, this little devil would change the way Europeans cooked for ever.

The chilli's popularity spread at breakneck speed. In the early 1500s, chillies travelled east with the colonial Portuguese, who took them to Persia and India. From there, they were picked up by the Ottoman Turks and, as these two empires pushed deeper into the world – west for the Ottomans, into Hungary and the Balkans; east for the Portuguese, into south-eastern Africa, Sri Lanka, Thailand and Indonesia – the chilli travelled with them, elbowing indigenous black and long peppercorns aside (curry, anyone?).

The chilli has transformed culinary traditions wherever it has grown. Here was an ingredient that was easy and cheap to cultivate, which brought with it anti-microbial qualities that proved invaluable both as a long-term preservative and as a device to make meat and fish safe in a pre-refrigeration world.

And, along the way, farmers selected and bred cultivars to suit their soils and landscapes, developing distinct chillies that gradually became more removed from their Mexican and Caribbean forebears.

We shouldn't think of this jaunt down the sixteenth-century trade routes as a finished thing. Food and ingredients travel still, though no longer in the ships and haversacks of merchants, adventurers and soldiers. Today, in Australasia, Europe and North America, we see the chilli travelling with immigrants who, by mixing their own culinary heritage with local produce, have reinvented flavour combinations and included the chilli in new food landscapes. In Africa, from north to south, the chilli has been used to spice up traditional recipes and, with more than three centuries of immigration, has helped to create bold and distinct cuisines across a continent. And everywhere, cooks and chefs continue to innovate, fusing together different cuisines and culinary heritages to create new ideas and recipes, just as their ancestors did before them.

Many of the recipes in this book demonstrate curious facets of the chilli's travels, revealing factoids of history and culture and reiterating that food cannot exist in a vacuum, divorced both from the people who make it and from their stories. The map overleaf gives some idea of how chillies have criss-crossed human history: our craving for spice and flavour resulted in a Spanish South America, the Portuguese slave trade, the British East India Company – and thus the British Empire. All because Europeans wanted to bring down the price of pepper. Our culinary desires truly have shaped the world.

THE END?
(14)

TURN THE
PAGE TO READ
ABOUT EACH
STOP ON THE
CHILLI'S GLOBAL
ADVENTURES

(1) The first stop on the chilli's travels is Darkest Peru, where archaeologists have found the earliest examples of agriculture in the Americas, dating back about 7,000 years. And right in the heart of the evidence, there's the chilli – spreading from its Mexican birthplace at a rate of knots. Exactly how this process of domestication and cultivation began is a big question, right on the cutting edge of ethnobiological research. But the chilli's place as the cornerstone of pre-Columbian farming is shown in pottery and art across ancient South and Central America. And as people moved, through trade or war, the chilli moved too, spreading rapidly across the Americas. (See Ricardo's Sea Bass Ceviche, page 37.)

(2) By the time Columbus landed on Hispaniola (the island of modern Haiti and the Dominican Republic), the chilli was already well established across the Caribbean and widely used in local cooking. In his first letter from the Americas to the King and Queen of Spain (which, without a postal service, he probably had to deliver himself), Columbus said that the locals' food had 'many spices which are far too hot': not an unusual reaction to proper Caribbean spicing. (See Middle Quarters Shrimp, page 24.)

(3) Is the Padrón pepper the first properly European varietal of chilli? Or is it a transplanted cultivar? Legend has it that the Padrón pepper was brought to Spain by Franciscan monks some time in the sixteenth century and that it was prized as an aphrodisiac, though exactly what the monks were doing monkeying around with an aphrodisiac, God only knows. No matter: the Padrón is uniquely adapted to the local soil of Herbón, where, on the first Sunday of August every year, they hold the *Festa do Pemento de Herbón en Padrón*. As the Galicians say, '*Os pementos de Padrón, uns pican e outros non*': 'Padrón peppers – some are hot, some are not'. (See Padrón Peppers, page 40.)

(4) Until about 1600, the Spanish and Portuguese held an almost total monopoly on ocean-going international trade – they had, after all, divided the world between them with the Treaty of Tordesillas in 1494. While the Spanish pushed into the Americas through the

Caribbean, the Portuguese went further south, first to Brazil, then to West Africa, seeking slaves for their New World plantations and introducing chillies as they went. (See Yinka's Chicken, page 60.)

(5) The Portuguese reached India in 1498, and took Goa in 1510. Their impact on its cuisine is profound. This is almost certainly the chilli's entry point to India and many Goan dishes reveal a Portuguese–Indian fusion, typified by vindaloo, whose name is said to derive from the Portuguese words for wine and garlic. (See Goan Pork Vindaloo, page 68.)

(6) Chillies came to Central Europe with the armies of the Ottoman Empire. Under Suleiman the Magnificent, the Turks conquered Belgrade in 1521, pushing north into Hungary from there. They left paprika – or 'the little pepper' – behind them. But where did they find it? Chilli authority Jean Andrews thinks the Turks discovered it when they besieged Portuguese Ormuz in 1513. So the chilli had crossed the Atlantic, rounded Africa, travelled back across Arabia to Anatolia, and found its way to the heart of Europe in just under 30 years, since leaving home in 1492. To look at it in a modern light, that's about as fast as our adoption of the internet. (See Veal Stew, page 71.)

(7) Aleppo sits at the western end of the Silk Road and has been, since its foundations, one of the principal trading cities of the Near East. Its souk, tragically destroyed by fire in 2012, was packed with spices of all kinds. So it's fitting that there should be a chilli named after it. From here, who knows how far chilli peppers travelled down the ancient caravan roads to the east? (See Omar's Chicken, page 109.)

(8) Arab and Indian spicers plied their trade along the coasts of Thailand, Malaysia and Indonesia long before the Portuguese reached Siam in the 1500s. So it's perfectly possible that the chilli arrived in the region via the ancient trade routes, in return for the cardamom and nutmeg sent to the Middle and Near East

CONTINUED ▶

since time immemorial. However it travelled, the chilli changed South-East Asian food beyond all recognition. (See Talad Pran Green Curry, page 62.)

(9) The Portuguese reached China in the early 1500s and eventually obtained rights to develop Macau as an anchorage and trading post. So, true to form, they're the most likely people to have introduced the chilli to China. But... it's a big place. If we keep in mind that, in limiting European access to trade goods from China and India, the Ottomans forced Spain to look west for spice in the first place, it would be a small slice of global irony to imagine that they in turn traded chillies into China down the very Silk Road they had closed to the west. (See Szechuan Aubergines, page 103.)

(10) Historically, the chilli's journey isn't pretty. Its spread through the Med was driven by the brutal wars between the Spanish and Ottoman Empires. From the Sieges of Rhodes and Malta to the decisive Battle of Lepanto in 1571, their navies fought their way from one end of the sea to the other. And by the end of it, the chilli had spread across Southern Europe and North Africa, leaving a culinary legacy and local varietals from the Basque Country to the Euphrates basin. (See Grilled Sardines with Maras Pepper and Pine Nuts, page 128.)

(11) Koreans like to claim that theirs is the hottest cuisine in the world. But the Korean Peninsula was probably the chilli's last stop in Asia, and one it made without the Europeans. By 1543, the Portuguese had reached Japan, bringing chillies with them. But it seems it was the Japanese who then took chillies to Korea when they invaded in 1592. In just 100 years, this little fruit had colonised the world. (See Cucumber Kimchee, page 212.)

(12) No one knows exactly when the chilli crossed from Mexico into Texas, but, at some point afterwards, it turned right and made a home for itself in Louisiana, where it was warmly embraced by the French settlers of the eighteenth century. Welcome to Cajun food – which would not be Cajun food without the bell pepper.

Along with onions and celery, it's one of the Holy Trinity of Cajun cooking. With its lack of heat, it's all too easy to forget the bell pepper's place in the chilli's adventure, but it's as much a chilli as the fearsome cayenne, the powder of which spices so much of this cuisine, and the Tabasco, which left Mexico to become the star of its very own Louisiana hot sauce. (See Cornmeal Catfish with Louisiana Salsa, page 127.)

13 If you really want to see how the chilli bewitches a people, look no further than the United Kingdom, a nation with an unjust reputation for bland, benighted food, but somewhere that has become, in recent years, a culinary Mecca. The British have always been early adopters of spice. A jaunt through Tudor and Jacobean recipes shows all sorts of interesting and unusual spicing, though, more often than not, they used mustard to bring the heat. In post-colonial days, the chilli has played an increasingly important role in the British food repetoire, which is influenced by those arriving or returning from India, Pakistan, Africa and the Caribbean, to name but a few chilli-loving regions. British chilli farmers have been instrumental in creating yet more varietals, from the mild apricot – an almost heat-free habanero – to the infamous Dorset naga. (See Dorset Chilli and Apple Chicken, page 130.)

14 Despite the chilli's deserved reputation as a preservative, it seems that the British navy preferred to salt its meat and preserve its vegetables in vinegar and citrus. So it's unlikely the chilli reached Australasia with Captain Cook. It seems, instead, that it took Asian immigration to jump-start Australia and New Zealand's love affair with chillies. Local chefs have embraced the foods of Australasia's many different peoples and created a unique fusion of cuisines, pushing the chilli's use as an ingredient in exciting new directions. Until someone successfully grows chillies in Antarctica, there's nowhere left on Earth for them to go. (See Pavlova In Purgatory, page 180.)

MEETING PROFESSOR SCOVILLE
or HOW WE FOUND OUT WHAT'S HOT <u>AND</u> WHAT'S NOT . . .

When cooking with chillies, it's generally good to have some idea of how hot you want your finished dish to be. As a rule, we're not looking for pedal-to-the-metal heat, but a balance in which the chilli's piquancy is one element in a broader flavour spectrum.

That we can do this with any measure of accuracy is down to an American pharmacist, chemist, lab director, magazine editor, author and, I suspect, cook, Professor Wilbur L. Scoville, who created the chilli's heat scale while developing a muscle salve. Scoville and his colleagues knew that, when applied topically, capsaicin, one of the compounds that give chillies their pungency, increases circulation to the site of application. The right dose applied regularly to a sore area fools the brain's pain transmitters into no longer registering the original pain. But if the dose is too high, the capsaicin will burn the skin (which is why you should wear disposable gloves if handling very hot chillies – see page 18). So he needed a standard measure of capsaicin. He developed a subjective test, assembling a group of tasters, who were fed chilli samples increasingly diluted with sweetened water. By measuring the dilution needed to remove the burn, he was able to gauge the heat ratio of different chillies. Hey presto! Scoville units were born!

However . . . as we learn in *The Life of Brian*, we are all individuals. This includes the chilli, which means that some serrano chillies or African piri-piris will be hotter than others of the same variety. So each chilli will fall within a given range of Scoville units. The chart opposite covers all the chillies featured in this book.

But, when push comes to shove, the only way to find out how hot a chilli may be is to test it: snap open the chilli, making sure it's facing away from you so that you're not spattered by any juices. Dab the open surface with the tip of your finger and touch the juices to your tongue. This will let you gauge how much of the chilli you want to use. Remember that the heat is mostly found in the chilli's seeds and the white membrane, or placenta, to which they're attached.

Chilli	Scoville Units	Real-time Heat
Sweet Pepper / Bell Pepper	0	Zero
Romano Pepper	0	Zero
Piquillo Pepper	0	Zero
Aji Cachucha	0–500	Mild
Thai Banana Chilli (*prik num*)	0–500	Mild
Ñora Pepper	0–1,000	Mild
Hungarian Hot Paprika	100–500	Mild
New Mexico Chilli	500–2,500	Mild
Poblano Chilli	500–2,500	Mild
Padrón Pepper	500–2,500	Mild
Anaheim Chilli	500–10,000	Mild–medium
Ancho Chilli (dried poblanos)	1,000–1,500	Mild–warm
Kashmiri *Mirch* (red Kashmiri chilli powder)	1,000–2,000	Warm
Cascabel Chilli	1,500–2,000	Warm
Guajillo Chilli	2,500–4,000	Warm
Jalapeño Chilli	2,500–7,500	Warmer
Fresno Chilli	2,500–8,000	Warmer
Piment d'Espelette	3,500–4,500	Warmer
Chipotle Chilli (smoked & dried jalapeños)	5,000–10,000	Getting Hot
Thai Long Chilli (*prik chee fah*)	8,000–12,000	Getting Hot
Serrano Chilli	10,000–20,000	Getting Hot
Maras / Aleppo Pepper	10,000–23,000	Getting Hot
Chile de Árbol	15,000–30,000	Hot
Hari Mirch (Indian green finger chilli)	15,000–30,000	Hot
Thai Orange Chilli (*prik luang*)	20,000–30,000	Hot
Aji Amarillo	20,000–30,000	Hot
Tabasco Chilli	30,000–50,000	Hotter
Cayenne Pepper	30,000–50,000	Hotter
Trinity Chilli	35,000–45,000	Hotter
Rocoto Chilli	40,000–50,000	Hotter
Ciliegia Piccante	40,000–55,000	Hotter
Adorno Chilli	50,000–70,000	Very Hot
Tien Tsin Chilli	50,000–70,000	Very Hot
Etna Chilli	50,000–70,000	Very Hot
Thai Bird's-eye Chilli (*prik kee noo*)	50,000–100,000	Very Hot
African Bird's-eye Chilli	50,000–175,000	Super Hot
Thai Karen Chilli (*prik kalieng*)	70,000–170,000	Super Hot
Habanero Chilli	100,000–250,000	Super Hot
Scotch Bonnet Chilli	150,000–325,000	Super Hot
Pure Capsaicin	16,000,000	Explosive!

See also 'Know Your Chilli'
on page 214–17

USING CHILLIES SAFELY

WHERE YOU SEE THIS SYMBOL
NEXT TO A RECIPE, IT'S BEST
TO WEAR GLOVES

Since capsaicin and the other capsaicinoids which make up the chilli's heat are serious irritants, you want to take care when handling chillies. Some people recommend rubbing your hands with oil before working with them, to act as a barrier. But, while the oil does indeed protect the skin from the capsaicin's worst effects, it also makes you clumsy – particularly with knives. So, I recommend using disposable gloves instead. Throughout the book, I have included a 'gloves' symbol (shown left) to indicate the dishes where I feel this kind of protection is necessary, but this is just a guideline and I suggest you follow your own judgement, since everyone's tolerance and reaction to capsaicin is different. Also, remember NOT to touch your eyes, nose or any other, erm, *sensitive* body parts after handling chillies without first washing your hands THOROUGHLY. If you do happen to burn your skin, dipping the affected area in milk or rubbing with cut citrus fruit should help.

While we're on the subject, if you eat something that's too hot, don't immediately reach for a glass of water. It will only make things worse, as it spreads the capsaicin. Every chilli-eating culture has its own tip to cool the mouth, including plain steamed rice, the yoghurt or raita drinks of India and Pakistan, sweet things like honey or sugar, cooling fruits like cucumber and banana, or just a simple glass of milk. They all work. Don't forget that Professor Scoville himself used sugared water to douse the chilli's heat.

Finally, don't play with chillies. You could hurt yourself or others. It is, as I've said, a FIERY little fruit. Don't over-chilli your food – the chilli is there to enhance a dish and to allow other flavours to shine in balance with its heat and flavour. It's not there to provide a test of machismo.

In short: respect the chilli.

DRIED VS FRESH
(AND FIRE IN A BOTTLE)

All chillies are not created equal: they range from sweet and mild to brain-numbingly HOT. And . . . to make things really interesting, when chillies are dried and smoked their chemistry and flavour profile changes. The heat of the capsaicin, which is predominantly stored in the seeds and membrane, is still present in the dried pods, but the character and texture of the chilli changes enormously. This is nowhere more evident than with Mexican chillies, which even change their names when they're dried, as you can see on the Scoville heat chart on page 17.

Fresh chillies are bright and very flavour-forward – you can feel the heat on the tip of your tongue, as it were. Drying them gives them a toastier, mellow quality. It deepens the flavours, much as the drying of apricots, peaches and grapes does, and can bring out tobacco, tea, pine or chocolate flavours, depending on the varietal.

More importantly, drying is a great method of preserving chillies. It's as ancient as the plant itself. And because it changes flavours and textures so much, it's best not to substitute fresh for dried, or vice versa, in these recipes. Instead, try to keep a range of dried chillies in the kitchen cupboard if you have the space, and remember that fresh chillies freeze very well – their flavours stay sharp, even if the pod loses its shape.

There is also a multitude of amazing hot sauces on the market, which can add a quick kick to soups, stews, drinks, egg dishes and much, much more. Better yet, a bottle of the popular Tabasco (where would the world be without it?) is under 100ml, so I often carry one in my handbag to pep up any dull dishes I encounter on my travels (for which, read 'long-haul flights'). So try out a few different sauces to discover your favourites.

SOUPS, SALADS
AND STARTERS

FIG, MOZZARELLA, ORANGE ▩ CHILLI SALAD

SERVES 2 as a main course, or 4 as a starter

1 large orange (or 2 medium), peeled, pith removed and thinly sliced

125g (4½oz) mozzarella or burrata

4 small or 2 large ripe figs, quartered or cut into 6, depending on size

1–2 hot red chillies, seeded and finely chopped

leaves from 1 fresh oregano sprig

freshly ground black pepper

for the dressing

½ tbsp fresh lemon juice

1 tbsp freshly squeezed orange juice

½ tsp white balsamic vinegar

1 tbsp extra-virgin olive oil

½ tsp clear honey

salt and freshly ground black pepper

Bright, fresh and packing a punch, this is the perfect salad to start off a meal, not to mention a chilli-based cookbook. You need a chilli with a fair bit of fire here to contrast with the creamy mozzarella and the juicy oranges. Choose a spicy fresh Italian *peperoncino* like ciliegia piccante. But don't let a lack of them put you off making this – any hot red chilli will do.

Make sure that your mozzarella is at room temperature when you assemble the salad, otherwise most of its rich flavours will be masked by the cold.

You can serve this as individual portions if you like, or bring it to the table on a single sharing plate, which looks pretty and makes more of a statement.

First, make the dressing: mix the juices and the vinegar together in a bowl, and season them with salt and pepper. Add the oil and the honey, and whisk together until they're well emulsified. (You can also shake all the ingredients together in a jam jar, if you prefer.)

To assemble the salad, layer the orange slices on a plate. Tear up the mozzarella with your hands and scatter the pieces over the orange. Gently place the fig quarters in and around the cheese. Scatter the chilli and oregano over the top. Then drizzle with dressing, to taste, and a good grinding of extra black pepper.

MIDDLE QUARTERS SHRIMP

WEAR GLOVES
FOR THIS ONE

SERVES 4–6

1kg (2¼lb) raw prawns or crayfish, in their shells but deveined

2 tbsp vegetable oil

1 tbsp sea salt, plus extra to sprinkle

4–6 fresh thyme sprigs

6 Scotch bonnet chillies, seeded and finely chopped

1 tbsp cayenne pepper

1 tbsp distilled white vinegar

Middle Quarters is a tiny village about halfway between the glorious YS Falls and the south coast of Jamaica, and is famous for its 'peppered shrimp' – a local Black River crayfish, cooked in Dutch ovens over wood fires and seasoned with a serious dose of Scotch bonnet. You drive up to a stall, buy the shrimp in paper bags and enjoy them at your leisure – ideally with icy cold beer – peeling them with your hands and licking fire off your fingers. This recipe might result in a dish that's slightly wetter than you'd find at a Middle Quarters stall – it's impossible to replicate that fierce wood-burning heat in a home kitchen – but its upside is a piquant sauce to mop up with bread. It's fine to use prawns for this, since they're generally easier to find. But if you can get hold of crayfish, all the better.

Wash the prawns in cold water and set aside in a colander to drain. Then mix all the ingredients, apart from the vinegar, together in a bowl and add the prawns. Toss them thoroughly through the spices.

Heat a large flameproof casserole over a very high heat and, when it's so hot you think it's going to buckle, add the prawn mixture. Cook, stirring frequently, until the prawns are almost completely red – 3–5 minutes. Add the vinegar, and cook for a couple of minutes more, still stirring, until the prawns are completely cooked – they will all turn pinky-red. Serve hot or cold, as a snack or as a starter, sprinkled with extra sea salt.

YUM NEUA NAM TOK

GRILLED BEEF SALAD

SERVES 2, or 4 as part of a larger meal

350–400g (12½–14oz) lean steak, in one piece

2 tbsp *nam pla* (fish sauce)

100ml (3½fl oz) chicken stock or water

2 tsp ground roasted dried chillies or chilli powder (to taste)

4–6 Thai shallots or 2 large shallots, thinly sliced

1 lemon grass stick, trimmed and finely sliced (optional)

2 tbsp fresh lime juice

handful of torn mint leaves

handful of coriander

1 tbsp ground toasted rice (see Tip, below)

to serve

extra toasted rice

chunks of white cabbage

extra mint sprigs

TIP

For the ground toasted rice, toast a handful or two of raw sticky rice (or use jasmine rice if you can't find this) in a dry frying pan until golden brown and smelling nutty. Remove from the heat and grind to a coarse powder. Store in an airtight container and use to add nuttiness and texture to Asian salads. It keeps for months.

Nam tok is Thai for 'falling water', which some say refers to the sound of the meat's juices dropping on to the fire. The dish is very popular in north-eastern Thailand and Laos, where sharp, hot, salty flavours are predominant, and where there is an enormous crossover of food, culture and language. It's a variation of the more well-known *laab* – another warm, spicy Thai salad. But here, the meat is grilled rare and then tossed into a dressing that has been heated with a little stock. Ideally, serve warm with a pile of sticky rice.

Marinate the steak in 1 tablespoon of the fish sauce for about 30 minutes at room temperature.

Heat a griddle pan over a medium heat until very hot. Being sure to reserve the fish sauce used to marinate the pan, put the steak on and grill for about 2 minutes per side – ideally you want it cooked on the outside but still rare inside. If you prefer your meat well cooked, then cook a little longer. Remove from the heat and set aside to rest a few minutes. Then slice the steak fairly thinly on the diagonal.

In a small saucepan, heat the stock, reserved fish sauce and ground chillies or chilli powder. Add the meat and stir it through, adding the shallots and lemon grass, if you're using it. Stir through quickly, then remove from the heat and add the lime juice, remaining fish sauce, mint, coriander and ground toasted rice.

Taste and adjust the flavours. It should be hot, sour and salty. Turn out on to plates and serve scattered with extra ground toasted rice and sprigs of mint.

SPICY SEAFOOD SOUP

SERVES 4

6cm (2½in) piece of fresh galangal, peeled and thinly sliced

2 lemon grass sticks, trimmed and sliced on the diagonal

2 Thai shallots or 1 small shallot, peeled and sliced

2 Kaffir lime leaves, torn roughly

6–8 Thai bird's-eye chillies, lightly bruised/crushed

12 mussels or clams (roughly 125g (4½oz)), washed and de-bearded

100g (3½oz) squid, cleaned and sliced into strips

8 large, raw, peeled prawns, with tails

100g (3½oz) firm white fish, cut into pieces (sea bass, tilapia or monkfish work well)

3–4 tbsp *nam pla* (fish sauce)

3–4 tbsp fresh lime juice

to serve

handful of Thai holy basil leaves *or* sweet basil

1–2 Thai bird's-eye chillies, chopped (optional)

Nam Pla Prik (page 192)

This clear, fresh soup is a version of the more famous *tom yum*, the ubiquitous Thai seafood soup made with roasted chilli paste and herbs. *Po taek*, however, is a subtler affair, set off by whole bird's-eye chillies, lime juice and fresh galangal. Its simplicity requires the very best ingredients to make it sing.

Bring 1 litre (1¾ pints) of water to the boil in a large pot. When it reaches the boil, add the galangal, lemon grass, shallots, Kaffir lime leaves and chillies. Bring back to the boil. Add the mussels or clams first, followed by the squid and prawns, and the fish last. Bring back to the boil again and simmer for a couple of minutes over a low heat, until the seafood is cooked through.

Add the *nam pla*. Discard any mussels that have failed to open. Remove from the heat and add the lime juice. Taste and add more fish sauce or lime juice, if needed – it should be sour, salty and spicy, with a lovely herbal undertone.

Scatter in the holy basil and the chopped bird's-eyes, if you're using them, and serve with the *Nam Pla Prik* on page 192.

GREEN PAPAYA SALAD

SERVES 2, or 4 as a part of a larger meal

1 tbsp palm sugar

2 garlic cloves, peeled

1 tbsp roasted unsalted peanuts, plus a good handful to garnish

1 tbsp dried shrimp

3–6 Thai bird's-eye chillies, sliced

125g (4½oz) grated green papaya (approx. 200g (7oz) unpeeled weight)

5–7 green beans, topped and tailed, and roughly sliced (approx. 30g (1oz))

6–8 cherry tomatoes, halved

1–2 large Thai long red or other red chillies, lightly roasted

1 lime, halved (optional), plus lime wedges to serve

1 tbsp *nam pla* (fish sauce)

1 tbsp fresh lime juice

CHILLI FACT

Known in Thailand as *prik chee fah*, meaning 'chilli that points to the sky', these chillies come in red and green. They are 5–12 cm long and a little more than medium hot. Their role in Thai food is to provide less heat than a bird's eye, and a lot of fragrance. David Thompson refers to them as long green and red chillies in *Thai Food,* and so will we.

You can find this salad all over Thailand. It's incredibly popular, and each vendor asks exactly how you would like it made, balancing out its sweet-sour-spiciness to your specifications. That said, I've had two truly great *som tams* in my life, and at each place I have never seen anyone interfere – least of all me. Khun Nok makes hers at her grilled chicken stall in Chiang Dao in northern Thailand and Khun Oh makes hers on the road out of Chonnabot, further to the east. They're worth seeking out. In the meantime, I've done my best to combine the merits of them both here.

You will need a large pestle and mortar to make this, preferably wooden.

First, make the palm sugar syrup: dissolve the palm sugar in a tablespoon of water in a small pan over a low heat. Don't let it boil. When it's cool, strain through muslin or a tea strainer to remove any impurities.

Roughly pound the garlic, peanuts and dried shrimp in a large pestle and mortar. Add the bird's-eye chillies and pound a little more to release their oils.

Now add the papaya. Pound the papaya gently to soften, using a spoon to scoop and lift the ingredients, mixing everything together as you work. Add the beans, tomatoes, roasted chilli and lime halves, if using. Bruise them lightly with the pestle, then add the *nam pla*, lime juice and a tablespoon of the sugar syrup.

Mix everything together gently with a spoon, and turn the salad out on to plates. Garnish with the last few peanuts and a wedge of lime, and serve.

GIN THOKE

PICKLED GINGER SALAD

SERVES 4, or 6 as part of a larger meal

juice of 2 large limes

10 × 5cm (4 × 2in) fresh root ginger, peeled and cut into matchsticks

100g (3½oz) dried broad beans, lima beans or butter beans, soaked in cold water overnight

100g (3½oz) channa dal or split peas, soaked in cold water overnight

130ml (4⅓fl oz) vegetable oil for deep frying, plus 2 tbsp for shallow frying

1 tbsp besan or chickpea flour (optional)

2 large garlic cloves, peeled and sliced

300g (10½oz) white cabbage, finely sliced

2 tbsp unsalted peanuts (preferably skin on), toasted

1 tbsp sesame seeds, toasted

2 Thai shallots or ½ red onion, peeled and finely sliced

3 green finger chillies or bird's-eyes, sliced

2–3 spring onions, finely chopped (optional)

1 tbsp *nam pla* (fish sauce)

1 tsp sugar

small bunch of coriander, torn

This refreshing, tangy, lightly pickled ginger salad is spiked with lime and chillies. The deep-fried channa dal and broad beans add great texture to the salad, so it's well worth taking the time to soak and fry them. They also make a terrific snack to have with drinks, so don't worry if you're left with an extra portion or two! Salt the extra beans and dal while they're warm and dust with a little chilli powder. They will keep crisp for a few days in an airtight container.

In a small non-metallic bowl, squeeze the juice of one of the limes over the ginger. Mush together well, and leave for at least one hour, or until you are ready to serve.

Drain the beans and the channa dal or split peas and dry them as thoroughly as possible – this helps avoid them spitting too much when they go into the hot oil. Then heat the vegetable oil for deep-frying in a large wok over a medium heat. When it's hot, add the channa dal or split peas and fry for a few minutes until deep golden brown. The oil will bubble furiously when they first go in, but once settled down you will be able to see the pulses changing colour. Remove with a slotted spoon and place on kitchen paper to drain.

Repeat the process with the soaked beans. When they're cooked, strain the oil and decant into a heatproof container for reuse.

If you're using the besan or chickpea flour, heat it briefly in a dry pan over a low heat and stir until it goes a toasty brown colour. Remove from the heat and set aside.

Heat 2 tablespoons of vegetable oil in a wok over a medium heat. Add the sliced garlic cloves and fry until crisp and golden. Remove from the oil with a slotted spoon and set aside on kitchen paper for the excess oil to drain off.

When you are ready to assemble the salad, strain the ginger and reserve the lime juice. Mix together the cabbage, ginger, peanuts, sesame seeds, shallots, crispy garlic, chillies, spring onions and 2 tablespoons each of the fried dal and the fried beans. Mix together well. Add the juice of the remaining lime, the fish sauce and the sugar. Mix again. Taste, and add a little of the reserved lime juice and extra sugar, if you like. Then scatter with the toasted besan or gram flour, if you're using it, and the coriander leaves. It should taste sharp, a little sweet, and salty, with a nice chilli bite.

MISS INA WILLIAMS' CRAB BACKS

WEAR GLOVES
FOR THIS ONE

SERVES 6

500g (1lb 2oz) mixed crab meat, picked through thoroughly

1 onion, peeled and grated

2 garlic cloves, peeled and crushed

1 Scotch bonnet chilli, seeded and chopped finely

1 tsp Old Bay seasoning

1 tsp dried thyme

100g (3½oz) butter, melted, plus extra for dotting

good grind of black pepper

good grind of white pepper

pinch of sea salt

25g (1oz) breadcrumbs, to sprinkle

lemon wedges, to serve

Miss Ina Williams is the cook at YS, a farm in St Elizabeth Parish, Jamaica. She often makes these crab backs for family get-togethers, and they're a particular favourite of my husband. So, of course, I had to ask for the recipe. It's rich and well spiced with Scotch bonnet and Old Bay, an American seasoning mix you can find across the US or, elsewhere, in specialist grocers or online.

Ideally, you want to bake the crab mixture in the cleaned crab shells – hence 'crab backs'. They should be 10–12cm (4–5in) across. But if you cannot find any, large ramekins serve just as well.

Pre-heat the oven to 200°C, 400°F, gas mark 6.

In a large bowl, combine all the ingredients, apart from the breadcrumbs, and mix together very well. Pop the mixture into the crab shells or ramekins. Sprinkle the tops with breadcrumbs, dot with a little butter and bake in the oven for 20–25 minutes. Watch them carefully because they can easily burn!

Serve piping hot, with a lemon wedge on the side.

RICARDO'S SEA BASS CEVICHE

SERVES 4

for the *leche de tigre* sauce

½ tbsp freshly grated garlic (about 4 cloves)

½ tbsp grated fresh root ginger

35g (1¼oz) red onion, peeled (you'll need 1 red onion for the whole dish)

15g (½oz) chopped celery

35g (1¼oz) fresh sea bass

200ml (7fl oz) fresh lime juice (from 7–10 limes)

75g (2½oz) ice cubes

salt

for the ceviche

1 tbsp puréed or grated garlic

1 tsp rocoto chilli purée

½ tsp aji amarillo purée

340g (12oz) fresh sea bass, diced into 2cm (¾in) pieces

55g (2oz) red onion, finely sliced

55g (2oz) rocoto chilli, seeded and finely diced (or a jalapeño or serrano chilli if all you can get)

1 coriander sprig, chopped

sea salt, to taste

to garnish (optional)

micro greens

½ small sweet potato, peeled, boiled and cut into cubes

Ceviche is a popular seafood dish in Central and South America in which fish is 'cooked' with citrus juice rather than with heat. It's sharp and fresh, and spiked with chilli and herbs. This version comes from Peruvian chef Ricardo Zarate. It features two chillies that are pretty much unique to South American food: the fiery rocoto and the milder yellow, fruity aji amarillo. Pastes of these are available online.

This recipe also features *leche de tigre*, which translates as 'tiger's milk'. It's a classic Peruvian sauce for ceviche, which is said to enhance your libido, cure your hangover and generally shake up your life in all sorts of wonderful ways. Just note that the fish should not linger in the sauce – you want to serve this almost as soon as it's mixed, so make sure you buy the freshest sea bass you can.

First, make the *leche de tigre*: place all the sauce ingredients except the salt, lime juice and ice into a blender or food processor. Turn it on to a high speed and add the lime juice gradually. Then add the ice and the salt, to taste, until you have an emulsified sauce.

To make the ceviche, mix the *leche de tigre* with the garlic, rocoto purée and aji amarillo purée to make a smooth sauce. Note that you can adjust the amount of chilli purée here to suit your palate. Add the sea bass, onion, diced rocoto and coriander, and fold them into the sauce. Season with salt, spoon on to small plates with some of the sauce, garnish and serve at once.

CHILLI FACT

A mainstay of Peruvian cooking, the aji amarillo is a medium-hot chilli, but with a surprisingly mellow fruitiness. It's yellow-orange when ripe and can be found fresh, dried, canned and as a paste (but avoid ground).

CREOLE ROASTED BUTTERNUT SOUP

WEAR GLOVES
FOR THIS ONE

SERVES 4

1 medium butternut squash, seeded
and cut into 8 wedges, about 1kg
(2¼lb) in prepared weight

2–3 fresh thyme sprigs

3 tbsp olive oil

1 shallot or small onion, peeled and
finely chopped

1 garlic clove, peeled and chopped

¼ Scotch bonnet chilli, seeded and
chopped

1–2 bay leaves

1½ tbsp *poudre de Colombe* or
Madras curry powder

1.2 litres (2 pints) good vegetable
or chicken stock

salt and freshly ground black pepper

1 lime, cut into wedges, to serve

Creole cooking is distinct from Cajun, even though many people seem to use the terms interchangeably. Some say that Creole descends from the original European inhabitants of New Orleans, others that it is a catch-all term for the broader French-influenced food found in the Caribbean and the Gulf of Mexico, as in this recipe. And it often features *poudre de Colombe*, the curry powder of the French West Indies, which you can now find quite easily from a number of good spice stockists or online. This soup is rich and golden, warmed by the mellow *poudre de Colombe,* and shows how the Scotch bonnet can be used to bring a delicate fire to a dish.

Pre-heat the oven to 180°C, 350°F, gas mark 4. Place the squash wedges and the sprigs of thyme into a heavy roasting tin, coat with 2 tablespoons of olive oil, and season with salt and pepper.

Roast the squash in the oven for about 45 minutes to an hour, until it is soft and tender. Note, though, that this could take even longer, depending on the age and the dryness of your squash. Just keep checking on it until it's done. Set the roasted squash aside to cool, then scrape the flesh away from the skin.

Now, heat the third tablespoon of olive oil in a large saucepan over a low to medium hob. Sweat the onion in the oil until soft, then add the garlic and the Scotch bonnet, and sauté for a few minutes. Add the bay leaves, and coat with oil. Then sprinkle in the *poudre de Colombe* and cook until it's really fragrant. Pour in the stock and bring to the boil. Then add the squash and remove from the heat.

Blitz the stock and squash together with a stick blender until it's smooth. Be careful not to splash yourself with the hot liquid. Then heat the soup through for about 5 minutes. Taste and adjust the seasoning. Serve in bowls with the lime wedges on the side.

SCALLOP SALAD
with PINK GRAPEFRUIT, DILL AND CHILLI

SERVES 4

400 (14) pink grapefruit or pomelo, peeled and segmented

2 tbsp fresh lime juice

1–2 tbsp light *nam pla* (fish sauce)

1 tbsp palm sugar

2 Thai shallots, or 1 larger, peeled and thinly sliced

1 bird's-eye chilli, finely sliced

50g (1¾oz) water chestnuts, sliced

2 tbsp toasted coconut

1 tbsp deep-fried shallots

2 tbsp toasted cashew nuts

3–4 dill sprigs, finely chopped

small handful of coriander leaves

2 spring onions, green parts only, sliced

4 large scallops, halved if large

1 tbsp vegetable oil

sea salt and freshly ground black pepper

to serve

1 Thai long red chilli, sliced on the diagonal

coriander leaves

sprinkling of roughly chopped dill

This tart and spicy salad is a fresh New World spin on a traditional Thai dish, *yum som oh*, or 'pomelo salad' – a perfect example of how Australia has taken on the cuisines of all its many cultures, added a few ingredients and fresh ideas, and made them its own. The toasted coconut slivers and deep-fried shallots are available in most Asian grocery stores and are great additions to your store cupboard.

Place the pink grapefruit segments in a large bowl. Gently remove the membrane that surrounds each segment and break them up into smaller chunks.

Now make the dressing: mix together the lime juice, *nam pla* and palm sugar. Set aside.

Gently mix all the remaining ingredients, except the scallops and oil, together with the grapefruit to make the salad.

Season the scallops lightly with salt and pepper. Heat the oil in a large non-stick pan over a medium hob. Fry the scallops gently for 30 seconds on one side, then turn and cook for 1 minute on the other, until they're just done.

Quickly mix the dressing through the salad and turn out on to a serving plate. Place the scallops on top and serve scattered with the sliced Thai long red chilli, coriander and dill.

PADRÓN PEPPERS

SERVES 4, as tapas

3–4 tbsp olive oil
300g (10½oz) Padrón peppers
grated zest of ½ lemon
sea salt

These gorgeous green peppers come from the Padrón region in north-west Spain. They are so simple to prepare and fabulous as an accompaniment to a chilled glass of manzanilla sherry. A note of caution: the majority of these peppers have a rounded, sweet flavour . . . but, every once in a while (about one in fifteen), one comes along and stings you with its fieriness.

Heat the olive oil in a heavy-based frying pan over a medium-high hob. When it's hot, add the peppers – you may need to do this in two batches – and fry them, turning occasionally, so that they start to blister slightly. How long this takes depends upon their size, but it shouldn't be longer than about 5 minutes.

Remove the pan from the heat and scoop the peppers on to kitchen paper for a couple of seconds to remove the oil, then put them on to a platter. Sprinkle with plenty of sea salt and the lemon zest, and serve immediately.

CHILLI AND SPINACH GNUDI
in A FRESH TOMATO AND OREGANO SAUCE

SERVES 4 as a starter

for the gnudi

300g (10½oz) raw young spinach

125g (4½oz) ricotta, preferably ricotta de buffala, drained

25g (1oz) Parmesan, freshly grated

2 large pinches of dried chilli flakes

1 egg yolk

grated fresh nutmeg

2 tbsp plain flour, plus extra for flouring the work surface

salt and freshly ground black pepper

for the sauce

2 tbsp extra-virgin olive oil

60g (2oz) unsalted butter

2 small shallots, peeled and finely chopped (40–50g (1½–1¾oz) in total)

2 garlic cloves, peeled and finely chopped

16 cherry tomatoes, diced

1 tbsp freshly picked oregano leaves, plus extra to garnish

150ml (5fl oz) chicken or vegetable stock

salt and freshly ground black pepper

grated Parmesan, to garnish

Gnudi are literally naked ravioli – just the filling with no pasta 'clothing'. In Venice they are called *malfatti*, or 'badly made', due to their sometimes ragged appearance. They are light but filling, so this also makes a great lunch for two with a simple salad and a glass of chilled white wine.

First, cook the spinach in boiling salted water until it has just wilted. Drain thoroughly in a colander, squeezing out excess water with a wooden spoon. Set aside to cool, squeezing and draining any more water from it every now and then, until it is dry.

Once it's cool, chop the spinach, making sure that you leave some texture, and put it in a large mixing bowl. Add the remaining gnudi ingredients and mix together well. Cover and set aside in the fridge for at least 30 minutes, but up to 2 hours.

To shape the gnudi, remove the mixture from the fridge and flour a flat surface. With floury hands, form the mixture into large walnut-sized balls (there should be enough for 12) and roll them into elongated egg shapes. Don't worry if the gnudi dough seems sticky; keep the flour to a minimum here to make them as light as possible. If you *really* feel that you need more flour then add a tiny bit at a time . . . Then place the rolled pieces on a tray or board lined with non-stick baking paper, sprinkle with a little extra flour, and set aside in the fridge for another 10 minutes or so.

Meanwhile, make the sauce. Heat the olive oil and the butter in a small, lidded saucepan over a low heat. Add the shallots and cook until softened. Add the garlic and cook for a minute or so. Stir in the tomatoes to incorporate, then sprinkle in the oregano and stir again. Pour in the stock and bring to the boil. Simmer gently for a minute or two, then season with salt and pepper to taste. Turn off the heat, but put a lid on the pan to keep it warm. Also warm some shallow serving bowls.

CONTINUED ▶

▷ CONTINUED FROM PREVIOUS PAGE

To cook the gnudi, bring a large pan of salted water to a rolling boil. Carefully drop them in – it's best to cook the gnudi in batches, no more than 3 at a time. If you try to cook them all at once, you'll lower the temperature of the water too much, and they will take too long to cook. Cooking in batches ensures they'll be lighter. As soon as they start 'riding' the bubbles or rising to the surface, which will take 1–2 minutes, scoop them out with a slotted spoon and place in your warmed bowls.

Spoon the sauce over the gnudi. Finish with plenty of freshly grated Parmesan, a good grinding of black pepper and a few oregano leaves.

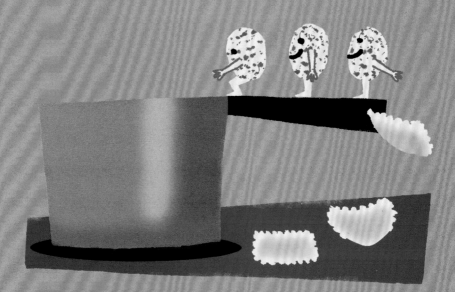

CHILLI GAZPACHO

SERVES 4

1kg (2¼lb) tomatoes, peeled and seeded

2–3 slices white country-style bread, crusts removed (approx. 125g (4½oz) after crusts off)

1 onion, peeled and roughly chopped

2 garlic cloves, peeled and smashed

1 hot red chilli, seeded and chopped

2 tsp hot smoked paprika

1 red pepper, seeded and diced

½ green pepper, seeded and diced

1 Persian cucumber or about ½ large cucumber (approx. 150g (5½oz)), peeled, seeded and diced

2 tbsp sherry vinegar

75ml (2½fl oz) olive oil

squeeze of fresh lemon or lime juice

5–6 ice cubes

sea salt and freshly ground black pepper

to garnish

1–2 thick slices white country-style bread, crusts removed (approx. 100g (3½oz) after crusts off)

4 tbsp olive oil, plus a little extra to drizzle

1 garlic clove, peeled and finely chopped

fresh basil leaves, torn roughly

As a teenager, I'd sail with my family from Malta to Sicily every summer. We'd sleep under the stars and barter beer in exchange for fish when we put into port. On these trips, this refreshing chilled soup would become an absolute staple as soon as we'd stocked up on produce. The fresh chillies add vibrant heat, offsetting the coldness of the soup, while the hot smoked paprika adds a mellow backdrop for the sweet tomatoes and peppers. Use the ripest, juiciest tomatoes you can find, and serve the soup as icy as possible.

In a large bowl, mix together the tomatoes, bread, onions, garlic, fresh chilli and the paprika, and set aside.

Then, in a separate bowl, mix together the red and green peppers and the cucumbers. Remove 2 tablespoons of this mixture, and set that aside to garnish the soup.

Add the rest of the peppers and cucumber to the tomato mixture, then add the sherry vinegar. Blitz it all together in a blender or food processor – you may need to do this in batches. You want some texture in the soup, so don't overdo it. Add the olive oil and lemon juice, stir through gently, and season with salt and pepper to taste. Place in a large bowl and add 5–6 ice cubes. Then put it in the fridge for a couple of hours, until you're ready to serve.

Meanwhile, for the garnish, cut the remaining bread into twelve 2cm (¾in) cubes. Put them in a bowl with the olive oil and the garlic. Let them sit for about 20 minutes or so. Then heat a dry non-stick frying pan over a medium heat. Add the oil-soaked bread, turning with a wooden spatula until crisp and brown on all sides. Set aside on kitchen paper to drain and cool.

When you're ready to serve, ladle the soup into four bowls. If it seems a little too thick, just add a splash of icy water to thin it. Top with the croutons, the reserved diced peppers and cucumber, and the torn basil. Finish with a drizzle of olive oil and serve.

CUBAN BLACK BEAN SOUP

SERVES 6–8

500g (17 ½ oz) dried black beans

2 bay leaves

2¼–3 litres (4 pints – 5 pints, 5 fl.oz) vegetable stock or water, plus a bit extra for topping up

4 tbsp olive oil

4–6 aji cachucha chillies or 1 green pepper, seeded and finely chopped

1 onion, peeled and finely chopped

4 garlic cloves, peeled and finely chopped

1 jalapeño chilli, seeded and chopped

2 tsp cumin powder

2 tsp dried oregano

3 tsp sugar

1 tbsp red wine vinegar

sea salt and freshly ground black pepper

to garnish (optional)

lime wedges

slices of avocado

chopped coriander

chicharones (pork scratchings)

Cuba has a rich food culture with deep Spanish and African influences. Its seasoning tends to be milder than much of the rest of the Caribbean, and more aromatic. This silky and substantial black bean soup really captures its balanced use of herbs and spices. My version is entirely meat-free, but if you want to acknowledge its proper porkiness, you should crumble some crispy bacon on top.

Rinse the beans and pick out any stones. Place in a large bowl with one of the bay leaves. Soak them in 2 litres (3½ pints) of water overnight (at least 6 hours but no more than 12) or put them in a large, lidded pan, cover with the same amount of water and bring to the boil. Simmer for 2 minutes then turn off the heat, cover the pot and leave to sit for 1 hour.

Strain the beans, rinse them and discard the bay leaf. If you have soaked your beans overnight, place them in a large, lidded saucepan. If you are making the quick version and have simmered them briefly, then return them to the same pan and cover with 2¼ litres (4 pints) of water or stock. Add the remaining bay leaf. Bring to the boil, then turn down to a simmer. Simmer, partially covered, for 1–1½ hours, or until the beans are tender but still with some texture. You may need to top up the liquid every now and then. Once the beans are cooked, remove the pan from the heat and remove the lid.

Heat the olive oil in a frying pan over a medium heat and add the chopped green pepper or aji cachucha, onion, garlic and jalapeño. Cook, stirring every now and then, until all the vegetables have softened – about 8–10 minutes or so. Add the cumin and the oregano and cook for another minute or so. Remove from the heat and set aside to cool briefly.

Place the onion mixture in a blender with 4 tablespoons of water or stock and 4 tablespoons of the cooked beans and their liquid. Blitz until smooth. Add this to the pan of beans. Add the sugar, vinegar,

CHILLI FACT

The aji cachucha chilli featured here is a mild, Cuban habanero chilli. It has a mild sweet flavor. And it ranges from green to orange, looking remarkably like its hotter habanero cousins. So take care not to get caught out!

salt and pepper. Bring back to a simmer, cover, and allow to cook for another 30 minutes. Remove the lid, and simmer for a further 15 minutes, or until the beans are really breaking down. Taste and adjust the seasoning as desired.

To serve, divide the piping-hot soup into bowls and garnish with your choice of avocado slices, a couple of rings of sliced aji cachucha or jalapeño, and chopped coriander. Serve with wedges of lime. It's also delicious with a streak of Maria's Fresh Tomatillo Salsa on page 198.

CURRIES AND STEWS

GREEN CHILLI
with PORK

SERVES 4–6

500g (1lb 2oz) tomatillos

2 poblano or Anaheim chillies

2 jalapeño chillies

6 garlic cloves

2 green serrano chillies

1 large bunch coriander (approx. 60g (2oz))

750g (1lb 10oz) pork shoulder, cut into 2–3cm (1½in) cubes

3 tbsp vegetable oil

1 onion, peeled and chopped

360ml (12½fl oz) chicken stock

1 tsp dried Mexican oregano (or normal oregano will do)

good squeeze of fresh lime juice

salt and freshly ground black pepper

handful of chopped coriander, to serve

TIP

Tomatillos are like large green physalis or cape gooseberries. They look like firm green tomatoes, each surrounded by a papery husk or outer skin, which is removed before cooking. It's worth seeking out fresh tomatillos, but if you can't get them, tinned ones work very well instead.

This Mexican dish has a fascinating interplay between the tart tomatillos, the deep, savoury qualities of the different chillies, and the sweetness of the pork. Each element has its role to play. None of the chillies is especially hot, but together they create an intriguing combination of flavour.

If you can't find poblanos, you can replace them with green bell peppers, and the other chillies can be replaced with any mild to medium green chilli. But it's really worth the effort to source the right chillies for this recipe if you can.

Pre-heat the oven to 220°C, 425°F, gas mark 7.

If using fresh tomatillos, remove their papery outer skins or husks and wash them well – you may find a sticky residue on them, so just give them an extra wipe with damp kitchen paper. Cut them in half and place into a non-stick roasting tin or one lined with foil.

Slice the poblano, jalapeño and (if using) Santa Fe chillies in half lengthways and add to the tin. Add 4 of the garlic cloves, in their skins. Season with salt, and roast in the oven for 20–25 minutes, or until all are softened and the skins lightly charred or blackened. Remove from the oven and set aside to cool.

If you're using tinned tomatillos, drain them of their liquid and roast the chillies and garlic on their own, as above.

When cool enough to handle, gently peel and seed the chillies and slip the garlic cloves out of their skins. Pop them in a blender with the tomatillos, roasted or tinned (they get to keep their skins), the fresh serranos and the coriander. Pulse until you get a nice thick sauce with a few chunks. Set aside. Tinned tomatillos may break down faster, so proceed gradually to achieve the texture you prefer.

Note that, at this point, if you simply season with lime juice and salt, you have a delicious Mexican salsa verde to use as you please.

CONTINUED ▷

CONTINUED FROM PREVIOUS PAGE

Season the cubed pork with salt and pepper. Heat 2 tablespoons of the vegetable oil in a large frying pan over a medium hob and brown the meat (you may need to do this in batches) until sealed and golden. Remove from the pan and set aside.

In the same pan, add the remaining tablespoon of oil and fry the chopped onion and the 2 remaining cloves of garlic (peeled and chopped) for 5–6 minutes, until soft. In a large, lidded saucepan, mix the onions, garlic and pork to combine. Add the chile verde sauce, the chicken stock and the oregano. Bring up to the boil and then turn down to a very low simmer and cook, partially covered, for about an hour, or until the pork is tender – this could take longer, depending on your meat. Then cook for a further 30–40 minutes, uncovered, to reduce the sauce if necessary.

Season to taste with salt and pepper and finish off with a squeeze of lime. Serve garnished with chopped fresh coriander and with corn tortillas or rice and black beans.

MOLE ENCACAHUATADO

PORK TENDERLOIN
in PAOLA'S PEANUT SAUCE

SERVES 4–6

for the mole
3 black peppercorns
5 whole dried allspice berries
2 cloves
3 garlic cloves, peeled
200g (7oz) peanuts, without skins
1 cinnamon stick, about 4cm (1½in) long
3 guajillo chillies
600ml (1 pint) chicken stock
1 chipotle chilli in adobo
4 medium tomatoes
½ medium onion, peeled and chopped
4 tbsp peanut oil
pinch of sea salt

for the pork
2 tbsp vegetable oil
700g (1½lb) pork fillet
salt and freshly ground black pepper

Paola Briseño is an outstanding young Mexican cook who leads food tours to her native Puerto Vallarta, and this peanut mole ('mole' meaning, simply, 'sauce') is a typical example of her cooking: warming, spicy and packed with flavour. Here, it's used to dress pork, but you could serve it over chicken, quail or grilled guinea fowl.

Pre-heat the oven to 200°C, 400°F, gas mark 6. Over a low–medium heat, toast the peppercorns, allspice, cloves, garlic, peanuts and cinnamon in a dry frying pan until fragrant (about 5 minutes). Remove from the heat and set aside, keeping the pan to use again.

With a sharp knife, cut a slit all the way down the guajillo chillies. Open them up and remove the stems, veins and seeds. Set aside.

Bring the stock to a simmer in a medium saucepan, and add the guajillo chillies, chipotle chilli, tomatoes, onions and toasted spices. Bring to the boil and simmer for 3–4 minutes over a medium heat, then remove from the heat and allow to cool for a few minutes. Transfer to a blender and purée until smooth.

Heat a roasting tin over a medium hob. Add 2 tablespoons of vegetable oil and, when it's hot, brown the pork fillet on all sides. Then bake in the oven for 12–15 minutes, until cooked through. Set aside to rest while you finish the sauce.

In the pan used for the spices, heat the peanut oil over a medium hob. Add the sauce, lower the heat and simmer gently for about 20 minutes, until thickened and reduced. Season with salt and pepper to taste. Cut the pork into 1cm (½in) slices, and serve with the sauce poured over the top.

CHILLI FACT
The guajillo chillies used here are actually dried mirasol chillies (*mirasol* translates as 'looking at the sun', describing the way they grow) and taste mild and lightly fruity, with an almost tea-like finish.

GOLDEN VEGETABLE TAGINE

SERVES 4–6

2 tbsp olive oil

1 onion, peeled and chopped

2 garlic cloves, peeled and chopped

1 large cinnamon stick, broken in two

1 tsp ground cumin

1 tsp cayenne pepper

1 tsp paprika

1 tbsp lightly crushed cardamom pods

1 tsp lightly crushed coriander seeds

1 tbsp ras el hanout

500ml (18fl oz) vegetable stock

800g (1lb 12oz) peeled butternut squash cubes, about 2cm (1¾in) in size (from 1 medium squash, about 1kg (2¼lb) before prep)

large pinch of saffron

400g tin of chopped tomatoes

2 tbsp clear honey, plus extra to drizzle

150g (5½oz) dried apricots

400g tin of chickpeas

1 tbsp chopped flat-leaf parsley

1 tbsp chopped fresh coriander

zest of ½ lemon

sea salt and freshly ground black pepper

Traditionally, tagines are cooked in their namesake domed clay dishes, set upon open fires, but this one is a quick dish to do at home with just a casserole or heavy saucepan. If you have a tagine, by all means use it for this recipe, but make sure it is flameproof and not just for serving.

This recipe features, among other spices, ras el hanout, a North African spice mix containing ginger, paprika, cardamom and rose petals, along with other aromatics. It is easy to find in most supermarkets and online. Note that this dish is more about fragrance than it is about heat. If you want to add some fire, serve it with the Simple Harissa on page 192.

Heat the oil in a large casserole or heavy-based saucepan over a medium heat. Throw in the onion and cook until softened, for about 5–8 minutes. Stir in the garlic and all the dry spices, then add the stock, diced squash, saffron and tinned tomatoes. Bring to the boil. Add the honey and apricots, and bring back to the boil. Then add the chickpeas, season with salt and pepper, and simmer, uncovered, for 15–20 minutes, until the squash is cooked through.

Taste and adjust the seasoning, if necessary – the tagine should be sweet, mildly spicy and fragrant. Finally, stir in the parsley, coriander and lemon zest, and finish with a good drizzle of honey. Serve with couscous and harissa, if you like.

TEXAS HOLD 'EM CHILLI

SERVES 6–8

1.5kg (3½lb) beef shin, cut into 3cm (1⅛in) dice

3 tbsp vegetable oil

3 guajillo chillies

2 pasilla chillies

2 cascabel chillies

4 *chiles de árbol*

2 chipotle chillies in adobo sauce and 2 tbsp of their sauce

1 large onion, peeled and chopped

4 garlic cloves, peeled and chopped

1 jalepeño, seeded and chopped

1 serrano chilli, seeded and chopped

2 tsp each of ground cumin, chilli powder and dried Mexican oregano (or regular oregano will do)

1 tsp ground cinnamon

200ml (7fl oz) beer

800ml (1½ pints) beef stock

2 tbsp cocoa powder or grated dark chocolate

1–3 tbsp cornmeal or masa

salt and freshly ground black pepper

chopped coriander, sliced avocado and sliced jalepeño, to serve (optional)

The Kellys were Texans through and through, who just happened to live next door to us . . . in Bangkok. They introduced me to America's south-west and to Mexico when I was just 12, jump-starting my love for the food of the New World. A good 35 years later, it's an affair that shows no sign of abating. So this chilli is inspired by those early Texan experiences and by Texas Hold 'Em, the so-called Cadillac of poker, wherein each player is dealt two cards, followed by five shared community cards. Where the player makes their hand from seven cards, we make this chilli from seven chillies. Note that there are no beans or tomatoes here. It's Texan. Deal with it.

Season the meat with salt and pepper. Heat a large, non-stick frying pan over a medium hob. Add 1 tablespoon of the vegetable oil and brown the meat thoroughly in batches until it's a deep brown on all sides. You will need to add a second tablespoon of vegetable oil about halfway through. Then set aside in a casserole with a tight-fitting lid.

De-stem and seed the guajillo, pasilla, cascabel and *chile de árbol* chillies. Toast them in a dry frying pan over a medium heat for about 5 minutes, until fragrant. Remove from the pan and soak them for 20–30 minutes in enough warm water to cover. Then drain and put in a blender with the chipotles, adobo sauce and 4 tablespoons of their soaking water. Blitz into a paste and set aside.

Add the final tablespoon of vegetable oil to the non-stick pan, turn down the heat, and add the onion. Cook until just soft, then add the garlic, jalepeño and serrano chillies. Cook for another 3 minutes or so, until they are soft and really fragrant, then add the cumin, chilli powder, oregano and cinnamon. Stir together thoroughly, then add the beer. Bring up to a simmer, stirring gently to lift any residues

CONTINUED ▶

▶ CONTINUED FROM PREVIOUS PAGE

from the frying pan, then pour everything into the casserole over the meat. Now add the stock, cocoa and chilli paste, and season with salt and pepper. Bring the chilli to a very low simmer, then cover and leave to cook for about an hour, stirring occasionally. Then partially remove the lid and cook for a further 30–45 minutes, or until the meat is tender.

Now turn up the heat a little and add the cornmeal or masa, a tablespoon at a time, stirring well after each addition, and cook it in until the whole chilli has a silky, rich texture. Cornmeal will give a texture to your sauce, while the masa will simply thicken it. I prefer the cornmeal, but it's a matter of personal taste.

Serve garnished with chopped coriander, sliced avocado and slices of jalepeño, if you like, and with the Cornbread with Cheese and Chillies on page 153 or with plain boiled long-grain rice. It's also terrific with Maria's Fresh Tomatillo Salsa on page 198.

CHILLI FACT

Cascabel is Spanish for 'rattle'. These chillies are so-called because they are plump and round, and the seeds rattle inside when you shake them. They're woody, smoky and medium hot.

CIOPPINO

SERVES 4–6

1kg (2¼lb) mussels, washed and de-bearded

2 tbsp olive oil

1 fennel bulb, chopped

2 onions, peeled and roughly chopped

1 celery stick, chopped

4 large or 6 small garlic cloves, peeled and chopped

2 tbsp tomato paste

1 tbsp chipotles in adobo sauce, blitzed

1 tsp fennel seeds

small bunch of fresh thyme

1 tsp dried Mexican oregano (or normal oregano will do)

2 bay leaves

½ tsp dried chilli flakes (add more if you like it HOT)

400g tin of chopped tomatoes, with juice

500ml (18fl oz) white wine

500ml (18fl oz) fish stock or water

400g (14oz) raw prawns (some shell-on and some shell-off)

600g (1lb 5oz) hake or other white fish, cut into chunks, or a mixture of white fish and salmon

1 tbsp chopped flat-leaf parsley

salt and freshly ground pepper

This is a take on the vibrant, spicy fisherman's stew, famous in San Francisco. The word *cioppino* is derived from the Genoese slang for 'chopping'. It is delicious, and just the thing for cold, dull, wintery evenings – a huge splash of colour and flavour to brighten up the weariest palate. The addition of chipotle chillies in adobo sauce is not traditional, but adds a smoky depth to the dish.

Sort through the washed and de-bearded mussels and dispose of any that stay open when you tap them. Set the rest aside with the fish and prawns.

Heat the olive oil in a large, heavy-based, lidded pan or deep casserole over a medium hob. Sauté the fennel, onion and celery until softened slightly. Add the garlic, tomato paste, chipotle in adobo, fennel seeds, thyme, oregano, bay leaves and chilli flakes, and stir to combine. Add the tinned tomatoes, wine and stock or water. Bring to the boil and simmer gently for about 30 minutes. Taste and then add salt and pepper. Taste again and adjust the seasoning, if needed.

Warm some big bowls, ready for serving.

Now add the mussels to the broth, bring back to the boil and put a lid on. Let them cook for 3–5 minutes. Add the prawns and fish and bring back up to the boil – these will cook really quickly, so don't overdo it. Another 3–5 minutes should be enough. Discard any mussels that haven't opened.

Check for seasoning, then ladle into your warmed bowls, sprinkle with the chopped parsley and serve with toasted sourdough on the side and a glass of rich white wine.

TIP

You can substitute any of the seafood, as you prefer, with crab, lobster, squid, clams or even oysters – you name it.

YINKA'S CHICKEN

**WEAR GLOVES
FOR THIS ONE**

SERVES 6–8

1 whole chicken (1.5kg (3½lb)),
jointed into 8 pieces

for the rub

½ tsp sea salt

½ tsp freshly ground black pepper

1 tsp cayenne pepper

1 tsp ground ginger

for the stew

2 tbsp peanut or vegetable oil

1 onion, peeled and chopped

4 garlic cloves, peeled and chopped

2cm (¾in) fresh root ginger, peeled
and finely chopped

1 Scotch bonnet, seeded and finely
chopped

½ tbsp coriander seeds, lightly
crushed

2 bay leaves

1 tsp chilli flakes (optional)

750ml (1¼ pints) chicken stock

400g tin of chopped tomatoes

1 tbsp tomato purée

340g jar smooth peanut butter

salt and freshly ground black pepper

to serve

handful of unsalted peanuts, toasted

handful of fresh coriander, chopped

lime wedges

At an English boarding school on wet and windy weekends,
we were encouraged to cook dishes from our various
countries. Yinka was from Nigeria and this was an absolute
favourite of ours: nutty, spicy, sweet chicken stew. It's been
a long time since she made it for me, so this version is a
recipe from the palate of my memory . . .

First make the rub. In a large bowl, combine the salt, pepper,
cayenne and ginger. Mix well. Add the chicken pieces and coat
them evenly. Then set aside for about 30 minutes.

Heat 1 tablespoon of the oil in a large, lidded non-stick frying pan
over a medium hob until hot. Add the chicken pieces a few at a time
and brown thoroughly, being careful not to overcrowd the
pan to ensure a crisp skin. You may need to do this in batches.
Once the chicken is crisp and golden on both sides, remove from
the pan with a slotted spoon and set aside.

Add the remaining tablespoon of oil to a heavy casserole and
heat over a medium hob. Add the onions and fry gently, stirring,
for 2–3 minutes, until they have softened slightly. Add the garlic,
ginger and the Scotch bonnet, and carry on stirring for another
minute. Add the crushed coriander seeds, the bay leaves and
the chilli flakes, if using. Stir to combine.

Now add the chicken stock, chopped tomatoes, tomato purée
and peanut butter to the casserole, stirring all the time; you want
the peanut butter to gently melt and amalgamate into the liquid.
Bring to the boil. Add the chicken pieces and any juices that have
accumulated. Bring back to the boil, then turn down the heat to
a low simmer and cover. Let it cook gently for about 40 minutes,
stirring every now and then to stop it sticking, until the chicken
is cooked through. Taste, and add salt and pepper, if needed.

Serve topped with a scattering of toasted peanuts, coriander
leaves and wedges of lime on the side. This dish is delicious with
mashed sweet potatoes, or plain boiled rice and fried plaintain.

**GAENG KEOW WAAN GAI
'TALAD PRAN'**

'TALAD PRAN' GREEN CURRY

SERVES 4

for the paste

12 green Thai bird's-eye chillies, de-stemmed

2 large Thai long green chillies, de-stemmed

1 tbsp finely chopped galangal

1 tbsp finely chopped lemon grass

4 tbsp chopped fresh coriander root, with some stem (see Tip, page 89)

2 Thai shallots, peeled and finely chopped

1 tsp grated zest of Kaffir lime (or regular lime zest at a push)

1 tsp *kapi* (shrimp paste)

½ tsp coriander seeds

½ tsp cumin seeds

1 tsp white peppercorns

good pinch of salt

for the curry

2 tbsp vegetable oil

400ml (14fl oz) coconut milk

350g (12½oz) boneless skinless chicken thighs, in 2cm (¾in) dice

2 tbsp *nam pla* (fish sauce)

1 tbsp sugar

100g (3½oz) pea aubergines

2 Thai round aubergines, quartered

100g (3½oz) bamboo shoots (ideally vacuum-packed in water), chopped

2 Thai orange chillies, each sliced into 3 pieces diagonally (optional)

large handful of Thai sweet basil

Nam Pla Prik (page 192), to serve

This classic Thai curry has gained a reputation for being mild and sweet, toned down over time to make it more accommodating to foreigners' picky palates. So it was something of a delight to taste the real thing at the Laan Took Dee, or 'Good Value Restaurant', in Pranburi, southern Thailand. It was exactly as it was meant to be: fresh and fiery, with no holds barred, transporting me back to the green curries I remember from my Bangkok childhood. And it made me fall in love with the dish all over again.

Chop all the fresh ingredients for the paste as finely as possible – this makes the next step much easier. Then pound them using a pestle and mortar – hardest ingredients first, working down to the softest – until you have a uniform paste. Don't worry if it's not completely smooth. If you prefer to use a food processor or blender, again work from the hardest to the softest ingredients. You also need to add a dash or two of water to bring the paste together.

Heat the oil in a wok or saucepan over a high heat and fry the paste until it smells fragrant – about 1 minute.

Add 200ml (7fl oz) of the coconut milk and bring to the boil slowly, stirring to dissolve the paste. Once it has dissolved, let the coconut milk simmer a little until you see oil appearing on the surface. Then add 200–300ml (7–10fl oz) water, along with the chicken.

Bring to the boil, then add the rest of the coconut milk. Bring back to the boil and simmer for about 6 minutes. Add the *nam pla* and the sugar. Taste and adjust the seasoning if necessary.

Add the aubergines, bamboo shoots and orange chillies. Simmer for another 3 minutes or so. Then add the basil and serve with jasmine rice and the *Nam Pla Prik* on page 192.

BRAISED CHILLI BEEF SHORT RIBS

SERVES 6–8

2kg (4½lb) beef short ribs, on the bone

2 tbsp olive oil

2 bay leaves

1 medium onion, peeled and chopped

3 garlic cloves, peeled and chopped

360ml (12½fl oz) red wine

2 chipotle chillies in adobo sauce, chopped

1–2 tbsp adobo sauce (from above)

1–2 tsp dried Mexican oregano (or normal oregano will do)

strip of orange peel

150ml (5fl oz) beef stock

400g tin of tomatoes

salt and freshly ground black pepper

lime wedges, to serve

In 1862, the French invaded Mexico, installing a heavily bearded Austrian, Maximillian, as Emperor. It did not end well for Maximillian, whose execution by firing squad was famously painted by Edward Manet. But even so, the story set free my culinary imagination, leading to this Mexican take on a French daube. The short ribs, cooked long and slow, have a dark richness and the chipotle chillies add warmth and depth.

Pre-heat the oven to 200°C, 400°F, gas mark 6.

Season the beef short rib chunks with salt and pepper. Over a medium hob, heat 1 tablespoon of olive oil in a large, non-stick frying pan. Brown the meat thoroughly on all sides – this should take about 20 minutes. Then transfer the meat to a roasting tin and add the bay leaves.

Add the second tablespoon of olive oil to the pan, lowering the heat a little, and fry off the onion gently, until soft. Add the garlic and soften that too. Then add the red wine and bubble it up. Add the chipotle, adobo sauce, oregano and orange peel. Bring to the boil and pour over the beef. Add the stock and tomatoes, then mix everything together evenly. Finally, cover the roasting tin with foil and place it in the oven. Immediately turn the oven down to 180°C, 350°F, gas mark 4 and cook for 3 hours. Then remove the foil and cook for a further 30–40 minutes to reduce the sauce.

When it's done, remove from the oven and skim off any excess fat. Serve with the Spiced Polenta on page 152, bitter greens and wedges of lime on the side.

CHILLI FACT

A chipotle is a smoked, dried jalapeño. The name comes from Nahuatl, the language of the Aztecs. The jalapeños are smoked slowly over fruit wood – sometimes apple, sometimes pecan – for a long time, so that they don't cook, they only dry. You can buy them either dry or tinned in adobo sauce, which is made with a range of chillies, cumin, cinnamon and vinegar.

CHICKEN DOROWOT

SERVES 4–6

for the *niter kibbeh*

250g (9oz) unsalted butter

2cm (¾in) fresh root ginger, peeled and sliced

¼ tsp fenugreek seeds

4 cardamom pods, seeds only

3cm (1½in) cinnamon stick

good pinch of dried oregano

for the dorowot

1 small chicken (1.5kg (3½lb)), jointed into 8 or 4 chicken leg-and-thigh portions, skinned

4 tbsp *niter kibbeh* (Ethiopian spiced butter, see above)

2 onions, peeled and finely chopped

4 garlic cloves, peeled and finely chopped

4 × 2cm (1½ × ¾in) fresh root ginger, peeled and grated

4 tbsp Berbere spice mix

500ml (18fl oz) chicken stock

250ml (9fl oz) red wine

juice of ½ lemon

1 tbsp cardamom pods, lightly crushed

4–6 hard-boiled eggs, peeled

salt and freshly ground black pepper

This is the quintessential Ethiopian stewed chicken, rich with *niter kibbeh* (spiced butter) and fiery-fragrant Berbere spices. The *niter kibbeh* is similar to a spiced ghee, and an essential flavour to the dish. Once you've made it, it will keep in the fridge for up to a month, and is delicious used to sauté vegetables, stirred into rice or pasta, or to finish a stew. Berbere spice mix, a pungent blend of cumin, coriander, cayenne, crushed chilli, ginger, fenugreek, cardamom and other spices, is now widely available in most stores and online.

Start with the *niter kibbeh* spiced butter. Note that you will need to strain it through a sieve lined with muslin and store it in sterilised jars (see method on page 193). Make sure you have both ready.

To make it, place all the ingredients in a saucepan over a low heat and let the butter melt gently; do not let it boil. Skim off any foam that rises to the top. Once the butter has melted, simmer until more foam rises to the surface and the white solids sink to the bottom. This will take up to 20 minutes or so – be careful not to let the butter burn. Remove from the heat and skim off as much foam as you can from the top of the butter. Then strain the clear liquid through the muslin-lined sieve, leaving the white solids behind. Store in sterilised jars in the fridge until needed.

To make the dorowot, season the skinned chicken pieces with salt and pepper, and set aside. Melt the *niter kibbeh* in a heavy-based casserole over a low to medium flame. Add the onions and cook until they're golden brown and slightly caramelised. This could take 20–30 minutes – just watch it carefully to make sure they don't burn. Add the garlic and ginger, and cook until well combined, about 30 seconds. Then add the Berbere spice mix and stir thoroughly.

Now add the chicken, and stir to coat it with the buttery onions and spices. Add the stock, the wine, the lemon juice and the cardamom pods. Bring to the boil, then turn the heat down to a simmer and cook gently, uncovered, for 1–1½ hours, stirring from time to time, until the chicken is cooked and the sauce reduced.

About 10–15 minutes before the end of cooking, poke each egg once with a fork. Then add them to the casserole and let them heat through and absorb some of the sauce. Taste, and adjust the seasoning, if necessary.

Traditionally, you'd serve this with injera bread, a sponge-like Ethiopian flatbread made from teff flour. It's delicious, and forms an edible plate at any Ethiopian banquet. If you have an Ethiopian food shop near you, you should be able to buy it there, or it's available at specialist online stores. Alternatively, serve with rice and greens.

GOAN PORK VINDALOO

SERVES 4–6

10–12 dried Kashmiri chillies

125ml (4fl oz) distilled white vinegar

1 tsp black peppercorns

1 tsp cumin seeds

2 tsp yellow mustard seeds

1 tsp coriander seeds

1 tsp whole cloves

1 large cinnamon stick

1 tsp cardamom pods, seeds only

2.5cm (1in) fresh root ginger, peeled and grated

6–8 garlic cloves, peeled and grated

2 tsp paprika

½ tsp turmeric

1kg (2¼lb) boned pork shoulder, cut into 2.5cm (1in) cubes

2–3 tbsp vegetable oil

1 onion, peeled and finely chopped

1 tsp brown sugar

400g tin of chopped tomatoes

salt

You can't have a book about cooking with chillies without including a Goan vindaloo. It's a classic Indian curry. All too often, eating it has been treated as a test of machismo by beer-swilling young men because it can be seriously hot. But it's also deeply fragrant and, done properly, it displays a profound subtlety of spicing behind the fire. This is a dish that really benefits from being made the day before you want to serve it so the flavours can develop.

In a non-metallic bowl, soak the dried chillies in the vinegar for about half an hour. Then remove the chillies, reserving the vinegar, and grind them together in a pestle and mortar with the black peppercorns, cumin, mustard, coriander, cloves, cinnamon and cardamom. Add the ginger, garlic, paprika and turmeric. Then stir the mixture into the vinegar to create a paste-like marinade. Rub the paste into the pork, and leave to marinate in the fridge for a couple of hours.

When you're ready to cook, heat the oil in a large casserole over a medium hob, and cook the onions until they're soft and golden. Now add the pork and its marinade. Cook for 5–10 minutes, until really fragrant, being careful not to burn the spices. Season with salt and the sugar, then add 360ml (12fl oz) of water and the tomatoes. Stir the curry together, and cook, covered, over a low to medium heat for 45 minutes to an hour. Then remove the lid and reduce the sauce until it has thickened. The pork should be tender but not falling apart.

Skim off any excess fat, then taste the sauce and adjust the seasoning. Serve with basmati rice and some chutney on the side, such as the Green Chilli and Coriander Chutney on page 199.

BORJU PORKOLT

VEAL STEW

SERVES 4–6

2–3 tbsp olive oil

1 onion, peeled and finely chopped

3 garlic cloves, peeled and finely chopped

1kg (2¼lb) veal shin, cut into 2cm (¾in) cubes

2 red Romano peppers, seeded and cut into strips

225g (8oz) cherry tomatoes (about 25)

pinch of dried oregano

2 tsp Hungarian paprika

1 tbsp tomato purée

500ml (18fl oz) veal or chicken stock (or enough to cover)

1 green pepper, seeded and cut into strips

salt and freshly ground black pepper

soured cream, to garnish

CHILLI FACT

Hungarian paprika is made from roasted paprika chilli peppers that are then sorted into eight categories from the very mild and sweet *csípmentes csemege* to the pungent and earthy *erős*. Hungarians say theirs is a richer red and slightly sweeter than its Spanish cousin.

Paprika is the spicy star in this very simple, traditional veal stew. The addition of Romano peppers breaks that tradition a little, but they enhance the depth and sweetness of the sauce. Adding the green peppers right at the end gives a little extra freshness.

Pre-heat the oven to 200°C, 400°F, gas mark 6.

Heat 1 tablespoon of the olive oil in a heavy-based frying pan over a low to medium hob, then add the onion. Cook gently until it's soft and translucent, then add the garlic. Continue cooking for another 2 minutes, until the garlic is just beginning to take colour, then set aside in a cast-iron casserole.

Now turn up the heat, add the rest of the oil to the frying pan and, in batches, brown the veal thoroughly. Set each batch aside in the casserole with the onion and garlic, and then add the Romano peppers, tomatoes, oregano, paprika and tomato purée to the casserole as well.

When you have browned all of the veal, deglaze the frying pan with half of the stock and bring to the boil, scraping up any cooking residues from the bottom of the pan. Add it all to the casserole, along with the rest of the stock and season with salt and pepper.

Cook in the oven for 30 minutes. Then turn down the oven to 180°C, 350°F, gas mark 4, and cook for a further 2 hours, until the veal is tender. If the sauce is still a little thin for your taste, let the casserole bubble over a low to medium hob for 10–15 minutes to reduce it down, stirring occasionally.

Finally, add the green pepper strips and return to the oven for a couple of minutes to heat through. Serve in bowls, garnished with soured cream.

CHAO LAY CURRIED CRAB

BPHU PAD PONG KARI

SERVES 4 as a part of a larger Thai meal

4–6 tbsp vegetable oil

8 garlic cloves, peeled and chopped

1 medium-sized onion, sliced lengthways

3 tbsp hot curry powder

1 large sea crab, cooked, cleaned and cut into pieces

400ml tin of evaporated milk

2 tbsp *nam pla* (fish sauce)

1 tbsp caster sugar

good grind of white pepper

1 tbsp chilli oil

3 eggs, lightly beaten

small handful of Chinese celery leaves (or normal celery leaves will do)

small handful of spring onions, cut into 2cm (¾in) batons

2 Thai long red chillies or large red chillies, seeded and slivered

The Chao Lay restaurant in Hua Hin stands on a pier jutting out into the Gulf of Thailand. I have been going there pretty much since it opened over 25 years ago – it's one of those places I will drive miles out of my way to visit – and I'm delighted to be able to share a version of their exceptional crab curry here. Its heat comes from the hot curry powder, while the eggy-creaminess of the sauce makes for a soothing and balanced counterpoint to the spice.

Heat a wok over a high hob and, when hot, pour in the vegetable oil. Add the garlic and onion, and stir-fry until fragrant, without letting them colour. Stir in the curry powder, then add the crab. Mix thoroughly to coat the crab in the curry powder, onions and oil. Pour in the evaporated milk and bring to a simmer. Add the *nam pla*, sugar and white pepper, and stir together.

Using a fork, mix the chilli oil with the eggs until combined. Add the egg mixture to the simmering curry and stir through. Scatter in the celery leaves, spring onions and the chilli, stirring everything through thoroughly. Remove from the heat and serve with rice.

GAENG HANG LAY

WEAR GLOVES
FOR THIS ONE

SERVES 4

for the paste

12 long dried Thai red chillies, destemmed

1 tbsp chopped lemon grass (about 1 large stick)

2cm (¾ inch) piece of galangal, peeled and finely chopped

pinch sea salt

2 Thai shallots, or 1 regular shallot, peeled and finely chopped

3 garlic cloves, peeled and finely chopped

1½ teaspoons kapi (shrimp paste)

for the curry

250g (9oz) pork belly, chunked

250g (9oz) pork shoulder, chunked

1½ tbsp Thai curry powder

good pinch of turmeric

2 tbsp pickled garlic juice

1 tbsp dark soy sauce

2 tbsp vegetable oil

7cm (2½ inches) ginger, peeled and finely chopped

1 -2 tsp nam pla (fish sauce), to taste

2 tbsp palm sugar

6 Thai shallots, peeled and halved (optional)

2–4 tbsp tamarind puree, to taste

1 tsp light soy sauce

6 heads of pickled garlic, peeled and cloves separated — chop them up if they're large

100g (3½ oz) roasted unsalted peanuts

100ml (3½ fl.oz) coconut milk

PORK CURRY
with PICKLED GARLIC AND GINGER

This rich, fragrant pork curry from the north of Thailand actually has its roots in Burma, demonstrating that food fusion is nothing new. There, it's made with a specific *hang lay* powder, which is difficult to find outside of Thailand. But Thai curry powder is similar and can be bought in most Thai supermarkets. Failing that, use a Burmese masala powder or your favourite Indian curry powder.

In a dry frying pan lightly toast the chillies until fragrant – no more than 30 seconds. Fill a bowl with boiling water and soak the chillies for 20 minutes, or until softened. Drain and dry well.

In a heavy pestle and mortar, pound the lemongrass, galangal and salt to begin the paste. Now add the shallots and garlic, and pound and grind the mixture until it's as smooth as you can make it. Add the chillies and pound again. Then stir in the kapi with the pestle to bring it together.

Mix the two cuts of pork together in a bowl with the Thai curry powder, 1 tablespoon of the pickled garlic juice, the paste and the dark soy sauce and set aside to marinate for 30 minutes if you have time. If not, just mix thoroughly.

Heat the oil in a wok and stir fry the pork until it begins to change colour, about 10 minutes or so. Add 300ml (10½ fl oz) water, bring up to the boil, then simmer over a low heat for about 25 minutes.

Add the ginger and shallots if using, and cook on a low heat, partially covered, for 25-30 minutes.

Now add the light soy sauce, nam pla, sugar, coconut milk, tamarind, remaining pickled garlic juice, the pickled garlic and peanuts and simmer gently, uncovered, for another 30–40 minutes. Add a little more water if it looks dry. Taste. It should be rich, sweet and salty, and the pork should be very tender. Serve with rice.

SRI LANKAN FISH CURRY

SERVES 4–6

for the Sri Lankan curry powder
1 sprig of curry leaves
1½ tsp black peppercorns
2 tbsp cumin seeds
2 tbsp fennel seeds
50g (1¾oz) coriander seeds
1½ tsp fenugreek seeds

for the curry
500g (1lb 2oz) firm white fish, skinned, boned and cut into 3cm (1½in) pieces
juice of 2 limes, plus extra for seasoning
1 tbsp tamarind purée
1 tbsp vegetable oil
1 small onion, peeled and finely chopped
3 *hari mirch* green finger chillies, split lengthways down the middle
1 garlic clove, peeled and finely chopped
6–8 curry leaves
1 tbsp Sri Lankan curry powder (see above)
½ tsp fenugreek seeds
½ tsp turmeric
1 small cinnamon stick
½ tsp ground black pepper
250ml (9fl oz) coconut milk
salt

Sri Lankan food is renowned for its spiciness, but this curry is relatively mild. It's also intensely aromatic, featuring its own unique and fragrant curry powder.

To make the curry powder, remove the curry leaves from the stalk and toast them with the rest of the ingredients in a dry frying pan over a low hob until really fragrant. This won't take long, so be careful not to burn the spices. Then remove and reserve the curry leaves and, in a pestle and mortar or with a coffee grinder, grind the spices into a powder. Mix the powder and the curry leaves together and store in a clean, sealed jar. This makes 85g (3oz) and will keep for a couple of months.

To make the curry, 'wash' the fish with the lime juice by putting them both in a bowl and giving them a good slosh around. Then drain off the liquid and add the tamarind to the fish. Leave to stand for 10–15 minutes.

Heat the oil in a heavy-based frying pan over a medium hob and add the onion, green chillies, garlic and curry leaves. Cook until the onion is soft, stirring often. Add the curry powder and spices, and stir them through the onion and chillies for a minute or so, then add the coconut milk, and season with a good pinch of salt. Bring to a simmer and cook gently for another 8–10 minutes, then add the fish and the tamarind. Simmer gently for another 5 minutes or so, until the fish is cooked.

Remove from the heat and allow to rest for about 5 minutes. Season with salt and lime juice to taste, and serve with rice.

STIR-FRIES, NOODLES, PASTA AND RICE

CHIANG MAI CURRIED NOODLES

DAD'S KOW SOI

SERVES 4–6

2 tbsp vegetable oil

4 large garlic cloves, finely chopped

4 heaped tbsp good quality Thai red curry paste

2 × 400ml tins coconut milk

800ml (28fl oz) chicken stock

650g (1lb 7oz) boned, skinless chicken thigh, cut into 2cm (¾in) cubes

1 heaped tsp turmeric powder

2 long dried red chillies

2 tbsp hot curry powder

2½ tbsp *nam pla* (fish sauce)

1 tsp fresh lime juice

1 × 'nest' of egg noodles per head, about 65–70g (2–2½oz) uncooked weight

4 tsp cornflour (optional)

to serve

4 Thai shallots *or* 2 small regular shallots, peeled and sliced

wedges of lime

extra *nam pla*

roasted chilli paste

fermented mustard greens

This is by no means a traditional recipe for this delicious northern Thai dish, but my father made it this way for years. He retired to a small island in the Med, where it's impossible to find all the ingredients to make an authentic paste from scratch. This recipe illustrates just what you can do with a few fresh ingredients and some store-cupboard staples.

Kow soi was one of my dad's favourite dishes, and it always reminds me of him. I remember travelling with him up to Chiang Mai when I was about six years old. He ate so many bowls of the stuff, I thought I'd have to take him back to the hotel in a wheelbarrow – it is that moreish! You have been warned.

Heat the oil in a large saucepan over a medium-high heat until hot. Add the garlic and stir-fry until golden brown, adding the curry paste and stir-frying until fragrant – just a few seconds. Add half of the coconut milk until the curry paste dissolves, then the rest of the coconut milk and the chicken stock, and cook until the sauce starts to reduce and thicken slightly. Add the chicken and stir well to coat, then the turmeric powder, curry powder, chillies, *nam pla* and lime juice, stirring well after each addition. Reduce the heat and simmer until the chicken is cooked, about 30 minutes.

Meanwhile, prepare the egg noodles according to packet instructions. Drain them in a colander.

If you're using the cornflour, dissolve it in 4 teaspoons of cold water, and add it to the *kow soi* during the last 5 minutes of cooking.

To serve, place each portion of egg noodles in a bowl and pour over a generous amount of the curry. Top with the shallots, and serve the wedges of lime, roasted chilli paste and fermented mustard greens on the side.

PAD THAI GOONG

PAD THAI NOODLES
with SHRIMP

SERVES 2, or 4 as a part of a larger meal

1 tbsp unsalted peanuts, plus an extra handful to garnish

4 tbsp vegetable oil

1 tbsp dried shrimp

125g (4½oz) rice stick noodles

hot water, to cover noodles

2 tbsp palm sugar

2 tbsp *nam pla* (fish sauce)

2 tbsp tamarind purée

4 garlic cloves, peeled and finely chopped

200g (7oz) fresh raw peeled prawns

2 eggs, cracked, not beaten

75 (2½oz) beansprouts

1 tbsp preserved radish, finely chopped

100g (3½oz) extra-firm tofu, cut into 1cm (½in) cubes

juice of ½ lime (1–2 tbsp)

½–1 tsp roasted dried chilli flakes

to serve

small handful of snipped fresh garlic chives or spring onion green parts

extra beansprouts

lime wedges

kreung proong (see intro)

For many in the West, pad thai, a stir-fried noodle dish, typifies Thai food. In fact, the dish is Thai-Chinese, and fewer than 100 years old in its current incarnation. It was created as the national dish shortly after the country changed its name, in 1939, from Siam to Thailand (meaning 'Land of the Free'). All kinds of tales abound about the whys and wherefores of it all, but suffice to say that it became a sure-fire hit with Thais and *farangs* (foreigners) everywhere.

This, like many other Thai dishes, is usually served with a quartet of condiments called *kreung proong,* consisting of caster sugar, mild chillies in vinegar, fish sauce and crushed, dried, roasted chillies, presented in individual pots. You can also serve with the *Nam Pla Prik* on page 192.

The best tip here is to line up all the prepared ingredients in order of use, then just work your way down the line.

Pre-heat the oven to 150°C, 300°F, gas mark 2.

Toast all the peanuts in the oven for 5–8 minutes, until they are nicely brown. Remove and set aside.

Heat 2 tablespoons of vegetable oil in a small wok, until it's very hot. Add the dried shrimp and stir-fry them for a couple of minutes, until nice and crisp. Remove with a slotted spoon and set aside to drain. This is not a traditional step, but gives the shrimp a lovely texture.

Pound the dried shrimp and 1 tablespoon of the peanuts loosely in a pestle and mortar – you just want an amalgamation, not a paste.

Soak the noodles in hot water according to the packet instructions. You want them soft and pliable but NOT mushy – remember, they get cooked further in the wok. Then drain, rinse in cold water and set aside to dry.

CONTINUED ▶

▶ CONTINUED FROM PREVIOUS PAGE

In a small saucepan, gently heat the palm sugar, *nam pla* and the tamarind purée with a splash of water until they have melted together to make a sauce. Remove from the heat and set aside.

Heat the remaining 2 tablespoons of oil in a wok. Add the garlic and stir until it is just fragrant. Add the noodles and stir-fry. Push them aside. Add the tofu and the prawns, and stir-fry until they are just cooked, push to the side. Add the cracked eggs and swirl them around the wok, then quickly add the noodles to coat, the sauce, the peanut and shrimp mixture, the prawns, tofu, beansprouts, pickled radish, and the lime juice. Stir it together rapidly, making sure it is all combined. Now add the chilli flakes and stir them through. Taste and adjust seasoning.

Turn out on to plates, sprinkle the chives, extra beansprouts and peanuts on top and serve immediately, garnished with a wedge of fresh lime and *kruang poong* (*see* intro) alongside.

TORN PASTA
with GARLIC AND CHILLI PRAWNS

SERVES 4

400g (14oz) lasagne or pappardelle

3 tbsp extra-virgin olive oil

2 garlic cloves, peeled and sliced

1 tsp dried chilli flakes or *peperoncino*

400g (14oz) raw peeled prawns, with tails on

50ml (1¾fl oz) white wine

zest of ½ unwaxed lemon

1 tbsp chopped flat-leaf parsley

salt and freshly ground black pepper

Puglia, spring 2002. There was a national strike, and our lunchtime flight had been postponed until the evening, so we were at something of a loose end. A very nice lady took pity on us, welcomed us into her (closed) café, and made this from what she had to hand: rough strips of home-made pasta and super-fresh prawns. We put the world to rights in a mixture of broken Italian and English.

This very economical recipe is a much more summery solution for using up those odd bits of broken pasta (which can mount up if you let them) than a *minestrone*. With its use of fragrant lemon, feisty, hot dried chilli and seafood, it tastes of that sun-filled afternoon on the shores of the Adriatic.

Break the lasagne or pappardelle into irregular pieces no bigger than 4cm (1½in) across. Bring a large saucepan of salted water to the boil, and cook the pasta according to the time on the packet, until it is *al dente*. If you're using lasagne, make sure you stir it regularly in the water to prevent the leaves sticking together.

Meanwhile, in a large non-stick frying pan, heat 2 tablespoons of the extra-virgin olive oil. Add the garlic. Cook for about a minute, and add the *peperoncino*. Then, when the garlic is beginning to colour, add the prawns. Stir them well into the garlic and *peperoncino*, season with salt and pepper, and cook them for a further 3 minutes or so, until they have changed colour and are almost cooked through. Add the wine, lemon zest and about three-quarters of the parsley, and stir together well, until the wine and the residual oil emulsify into a sauce. Then stir in the remaining oil.

Drain the cooked pasta and add it to the pan with the garlicky chilli prawns and sauce, stirring it through. Divide between plates, sprinkle on the remaining parsley and serve at once.

CAPELLINI
with QUICK SPICY TOMATO SAUCE

SERVES 2

3–4 tbsp olive oil

2 large garlic cloves, skin removed and lightly smashed

1 large tomato, chopped roughly into 6–8 pieces

good pinch of dried chilli flakes

200g (7oz) dried capellini

sea salt and freshly ground black pepper

to serve

good drizzle of extra-virgin olive oil

flat-leaf parsley, chopped

This is a beautifully simple lunch for two, and one of my store-cupboard favourites. The soft oil-poached garlic turns delightfully sweet, while the chilli and tomato add sharpness and piquancy to create a well-structured sauce that's packed with flavour.

Bring a large saucepan of salted water to a rolling boil over a high heat for the pasta.

Heat the olive oil in a medium non-stick frying pan over a low hob. Add the garlic and cook very gently for 3–4 minutes until it has softened and is just beginning to turn a light golden colour. Throw in the chopped tomato and chilli, and let them simmer away until the tomatoes start to break down – they should be soft and giving. Season with salt and pepper.

Meanwhile, cook the capellini as per the instructions on the packet. When it's ready, drain it well. Throw the pasta into the sauce and coat thoroughly. Serve in bowls, finished with a drizzle of extra-virgin olive oil and the flat-leaf parsley.

THAI-STYLE CHICKEN BIRYANI

SERVES 4–6

for the biryani powder

2 tsp coriander seeds

2 tsp cumin seeds

1 bay leaf

3 tsp Madras curry powder

1 tsp turmeric

½ tsp ground cinnamon

for the paste

6 garlic cloves, peeled and chopped

3cm (1½in) fresh root ginger, peeled and chopped

25 white peppercorns

1 large coriander root (see Tip), roughly chopped

1 clove

good pinch of salt

for the rest of the dish

800g (1lb 12oz) chicken thighs on the bone, skin on

100ml (3½fl oz) evaporated milk

1 tbsp caster sugar

1 tsp salt

1 cinnamon stick, broken into 3 pieces

8 tbsp vegetable oil

10 Thai shallots *or* 3–4 larger shallots, peeled and finely sliced

500g (1lb 2oz) rice

600ml (1 pint) chicken stock or water

8 Thai cardamom pods *or* 4–6 green cardamom pods, lightly crushed

2 bay leaves

large pinch of saffron

20g (¾oz) unsalted butter

juice of 1 lime

This is an Indian dish that travelled, packed with classic spice-route flavours, until – *CRASH!* – it hit the south of Thailand. It's typical of the kind of cooking you find all along the Isthmus of Kra, especially in the district of Takua Pa, which was a hub of the cardamom trade. The two dipping sauces included here (see over the page) are pure Thailand. The first is packed with bird's-eye chillies, coriander, palm sugar and tamarind. Fantastic flavours, certainly, but beware: it's seriously HOT! The second is a milder, sweeter, vinegar-based sauce. Serve them both.

First make the biryani powder. Toast the coriander and cumin seeds in a dry pan over a low heat until fragrant – a minute or so. Remove from the heat and grind the seeds with a coffee grinder or a pestle and mortar, along with the bay leaf, to a powder. Mix well with the rest of the biryani powder ingredients. This makes 3–4 tablespoons, and keeps very well for up to 3 months in an airtight jar.

Slash the skin and flesh of the chicken thighs and place in a bowl. With a pestle and mortar, grind the paste ingredients until smooth.

Mix the paste with 1 tablespoon of the biryani powder, plus the evaporated milk, sugar and salt, and pour over the chicken, using your hands to massage it all in. Add the broken cinnamon stick. Leave the chicken to marinate for at least an hour, preferably 3 or 4.

Meanwhile, heat 2 tablespoons of the vegetable oil in a wok over a high hob. When it's very hot, fry half of the sliced shallots until crisp and golden, always moving them around in the oil so they do not burn or stick. Drain with a slotted spoon and set aside. Discard any remaining oil and wipe out the wok.

Rinse the rice several times, drain well and set aside. Shake and scrape the excess marinade off the chicken, then set both the meat and marinade aside in separate bowls.

TIP

Coriander root is a key ingredient in Thai cooking. Its flavour is both mellower and yet more profound than coriander stem. It's easy to find in Asian stores, sometimes located in the freezer section. If you can't find it, replace each root with 3–4 coriander stems.

Heat the remaining vegetable oil in the clean wok and fry the chicken thighs, a few at a time. You want them golden on the outside and beginning to cook through. This will take 4–5 minutes per batch, depending on their size.

Once cooked, place them into a casserole dish or a heavy-based saucepan with a lid. Add the rinsed rice, the rest of the raw shallots, the chicken stock or water, cardamom pods, bay leaf and saffron. Add the remaining reserved marinade at this point, including the cinnamon stick, then the butter. Bring to a boil and cover. Turn down to a very low heat and simmer for 20–25 minutes, or until the rice has absorbed the liquid and the chicken is cooked through. Remove from the heat and stir in half of the deep-fried shallots and the lime juice, then put the lid back on the rice pot and set aside to rest for 10 minutes.

Serve sprinkled with the remaining deep-fried shallots and the dipping sauces on the next page.

CONTINUED ▶

CONTINUED FROM PREVIOUS PAGE

KHAO MOK GAI DIPPING SAUCE

1 large coriander root (see Tip, page 89)

8 garlic cloves, peeled and chopped

small handful of coriander leaves

12 Thai bird's-eye chillies, chopped

2–3 large Thai long chillies (green or red), chopped

2 heaped tsp palm sugar

3–4 tbsp tamarind purée

salt, to taste

With a pestle and mortar, pound together the coriander root, and chopped garlic until smooth.

In a bowl combine the coriander leaves, bird's-eye chillies, Thai long chillies, 130ml (4½fl oz) of water, the palm sugar, tamarind purée and salt. Using a stick blender, whizz all this into a sauce. Stir in the pounded coriander root and garlic and whizz again. Place the sauce into a small saucepan and heat gently for a minute or two, until it just starts to simmer. Remove from the heat and serve.

GREEN DIPPING SAUCE

8–12 green bird's-eye chillies

3cm (1½in) fresh root ginger, peeled

2 large spring onions, trimmed

handful of fresh coriander

3 tbsp caster sugar

3 tbsp distilled white vinegar

salt, to taste

Finely chop the chillies, ginger, spring onion and coriander and set aside. Place the sugar, vinegar, salt and a splash of water in a small saucepan and heat gently over a low hob until the sugar and salt have dissolved. Remove from the heat and allow to cool slightly, then stir in the remaining ingredients and serve.

HOY PAD NAM PRIK POW
BAI HORAPHA

THAI STIR-FRIED CLAMS
with ROASTED CHILLI PASTE AND SWEET BASIL

**SERVES 2, or 4 as a part of
a larger Thai meal**

500g (1lb 2oz) live clams

2 tbsp vegetable oil

2–3 garlic cloves, peeled and
chopped

1 tbsp *nam prik pow* (Thai roasted
chilli paste)

1 tbsp *nam pla* (fish sauce)

1 tsp caster sugar

2 red Thai long red chillies, sliced
diagonally

25g (1oz) Thai sweet basil leaves

This tastes so complex for a dish that takes so little time
to make. The sweet clams, rich chilli paste and fresh basil
create a perfect balance of flavour. If you can't find Thai
sweet basil, or *horapha*, regular basil works perfectly well.

In a colander, rinse the clams well under cold running water,
discarding any that remain open when tapped.

On a high hob, heat a wok until it's very hot and add the oil. Then fry
the garlic until it's golden. Add the clams and the *nam prik pow*, and
stir-fry for a minute or two.

Now add the *nam pla*, sugar, 2 tablespoons of water and the chillies,
one at a time, stirring them well into the clams after each addition.
Then continue to cook, stirring all the time, until all the clams are
open. Discard any that haven't opened.

Finally, add most of the basil and stir it into the clams and sauce
until it's wilted. Serve at once, with the last few basil leaves
scattered over the top and steamed jasmine rice on the side.

WILD MUSHROOMS
STIR-FRIED *with* HOLY BASIL

SERVES 2, or 4 as a part of a larger Thai meal

4–6 Thai bird's-eye chillies

1 large Thai long red chilli *or* Thai orange chilli, roughly chopped

10–12 Thai garlic cloves *or* 5–6 regular garlic cloves, peeled

pinch of sea salt

2 tbsp dark soy sauce

1 tbsp light soy sauce

pinch of sugar

1–2 tbsp vegetable oil

300g (10½oz) wild mushrooms, halved if very large

100g (3½oz) green beans, topped, tailed and cut into 1cm (½in) pieces

large handful of *bai krapow* (holy basil leaves)

When it comes to comfort food, I never think of things like bangers and mash; for me, it's *pad krapow*. It's the perfect one-plate meal: fluffy aromatic rice, topped with this fiery, salty, fragrant stir-fry, topped again with a deep-fried egg (see recipe for Drunkard's Beef Fried Rice on page 94), if you like. Heaven.

If you can't find Thai holy basil, you can substitute it with whatever basil you can source locally. Similarly, if you can't find Thai garlic – which has very small cloves with delicate skins – normal garlic will be fine. Just bear in mind that about two Thai garlic cloves equals one regular garlic clove.

Remove the stalks from the chillies and pound them with the garlic and salt in a pestle and mortar until they form a rough paste. Set aside.

Mix the soy sauces and 2 tablespoons of water together in a small bowl, and stir in the sugar.

Heat the oil in a wok over a very high hob. Add the chilli and garlic, and stir-fry for a few seconds, until fragrant but not coloured. Now add the wild mushrooms and the green beans, and stir to coat.

Now add the soy and water mixture. Stir through, bubbling it up hard. Then wilt the basil into the dish, reserving a few leaves to garnish, and serve with steamed jasmine rice and the last few basil leaves on top.

DRUNKARD'S BEEF FRIED RICE

SERVES 2

225g (8oz) Thai rice (uncooked weight), cooked and allowed to cool down (see intro)

125g (4½oz) beef sirloin or rump

1 heaped tsp *nam prik pow* (Thai roasted chilli paste)

1 tbsp dark soy sauce

2 tbsp *nam pla* (fish sauce)

1 tsp tamarind purée

1 tsp chilli powder

pinch of sugar

½ Thai long red chilli or any large red chilli, seeded

2 Thai bird's-eye chillies, seeded

2 large garlic cloves, peeled

2 large coriander roots (see Tip, page 89)

pinch of salt

2–3 tbsp vegetable oil

1 tomato, cut into 8

6 lime leaves, rolled and sliced

large handful of *horapha* (sweet Thai basil leaves), stems taken off

to serve

lime wedges

Nam Pla Prik (page 192)

2 eggs (optional)

vegetable oil, for deep-frying (optional)

This fried rice is said to be a great hangover cure, or that it should be eaten to prevent one . . . I've tried it both ways and, trust me, it certainly reboots the system! It's fragrant, spicy and oh so good.

Note that the two biggest mistakes people make when cooking fried rice are: a) using hot or warm rice – its moisture just leads to a claggy mess; and b) using chilled leftover rice directly from the fridge, which will end up tough and chewy. Have respect for the fried rice. It takes no time to cook some rice and set it aside to cool to room temperature while you're prepping the other bits. Alternatively, use cooled-down rice left over from a lunch to make a glorious one-dish supper on the same day.

If you can't find Thai sweet basil, regular basil will do.

Cook the rice according to the instructions on the packet and set aside to cool to room temperature. Slice the beef into thin strips and set aside.

In a small bowl, mix together the roasted chilli paste, soy sauce, *nam pla*, tamarind purée, chilli powder and pinch of sugar with 1 tablespoon of water. Set aside.

Using a pestle and mortar, pound together the Thai long red and bird's-eye chillies, garlic, coriander roots and pinch of salt, until you get a rough paste.

Heat a wok over a high hob, then add the oil. Add the paste of chillies, garlic and coriander, and cook for a minute until really fragrant, stirring all the time to prevent the garlic from burning. Then add the beef and carry on stirring for another minute or two until the beef starts to colour.

Now stir in the tomato and add the chilli/soy mixture, along with the lime leaves. Tip in the cooked rice and half of the *horapha*

CHILLI FACT

The Thais call their bird's-eye chillies *prik kee noo*, which means 'mouse poo chillies'. Be assured that's due to their size and shape and nothing else! Thais have a saying – *Lek prik kee noo* – which, roughly translated, means, 'It may be small, but it's still a chilli pepper.' It's often used to describe naughty children or feisty characters! But at 50,000 Scoville units, Thai bird's-eye chillies are not even half as hot as some chillies you might encounter.

(basil). Keep stirring until everything is combined and hot all the way through – this should take about 5 minutes. Stir in the other half of the *horapha* leaves, reserving a few to garnish.

Serve garnished with the extra basil on top, a wedge of lime and some *Nam Pla Prik* (page 192) on the side.

A nice, Thai touch is to serve a deep-fried egg on top of each bowl. Heat 2cm (¾in) of vegetable oil in a small wok, taking care to make sure it's stable, and, when the oil is hot, crack in an egg. Fry until the white is crispy and the yolk runny – about a minute. Scoop out with a slotted spoon and place it atop your *Khao Pad*.

KODI VEPADU

GUNTUR-STYLE FRIED CHICKEN STIR-FRY

SERVES 4

400g (14oz) boneless skinless chicken, cut into 2cm (¾in) pieces

oil, for deep-frying

for the spiced coating

2 tbsp gram flour

1 tbsp rice flour

salt

1 tsp turmeric

1 tbsp Kashmiri *mirch* (chilli powder)

1–2 garlic cloves, peeled and minced

2cm (¾in) fresh root ginger, peeled and minced

for the stir-fry

1–2 tbsp vegetable oil

1 onion, peeled and finely chopped

4–6 Indian green finger chillies, slit open

2 sprigs of fresh curry leaves, removed from stems

small handful of fresh coriander, chopped

salt

CHILLI FACT

Hari mirch, or the Indian green finger chilli, measures 15,000–30,000 on the Scoville scale. It's so easily available, it's almost as ubiquitous as the green jalapeño. It's renowned for its healthy properties – it's rich in vitamin A and packs in six times more vitamin C than an orange. Plus, it's said to bolster the immune system and aid weight-loss.

Guntur sits at the centre of India's chilli production. It is home to several distinct chilli varieties and is also the site of Asia's largest chilli market, exporting the hot stuff all over the world. So, given Guntur's place in the chilli firmament, there was no way I could possibly leave out this local recipe, which features both red chilli powder and fresh green finger chillies, called *hari mirch*. Note that the chicken *does* get fried twice in this recipe – you are not misreading it. For the roasted cauliflower, turn to page 148 and for the spiced green beans see page 140.

First, prepare the spiced coating. Mix the flours, salt and dry spices in a large bowl. Toss the chicken with the garlic and ginger, then in the spiced flour. Leave to absorb the flavours for about half an hour. When you're ready to cook, shake the excess flour from the chicken and set aside, reserving any excess flour, ginger and garlic mixture.

In a deep-fat fryer, heat sufficient oil to 180°C, 350°F. Alternatively, heat a depth of about 5cm (2in) of oil in a small wok over a medium heat. Make sure the wok is stable and safe. Deep-fry the chicken in batches until it's golden and cooked through, for 3–5 minutes. Remove the cooked chicken pieces with a slotted spoon and set aside on kitchen paper to drain. If there is any of the flour, garlic and ginger mixture left over, fry it with the last batch of chicken.

When you've cooked all the chicken, heat 1–2 tablespoons of fresh oil in a clean wok over a medium–high heat. Add the onions, stir them into the oil, then add the chillies and curry leaves and stir-fry until the onion begins to turn translucent. Season with salt, stir-fry for a further minute or so, then add the chicken. Stir-fry all the ingredients together thoroughly in the wok, then add the coriander. Turn out on to a platter and serve with rice.

FETTUCCINE
with GARLIC, OIL AND PEPERONCINO

SERVES 2

200g (7oz) dried fettuccine

2–3 tbsp olive oil

3 garlic cloves, peeled and coarsely sliced

1 ciliegia piccante chilli or any medium-hot red chilli, sliced

1 tbsp chopped flat-leaf parsley

salt and freshly ground black pepper

grated Parmesan, to serve

This is about as simple a dish as you can imagine, which is the key to its magnificence, so make sure you use the best ingredients you can. I've chosen ciliegia piccante chillies because, though their fruits aren't sold commercially, their seeds and plants are easy to find. It's a southern Italian variety that looks halfway between a bright red cherry and a plum, has a softer warmth and delicious fruity tones. But don't let access to the chillies stop you cooking this – if you can't find them, replace them with the fresh medium-hot red chilli of your choice.

Cook the pasta as per its instructions, until it reaches your preferred texture. (Everyone talks about the perfect pasta being cooked *al dente*, but I've yet to meet two people who can agree on what *al dente* is. It's a subjective matter of preference. We're talking cooked enough not to give you indigestion, but not so cooked that you can use it in place of wallpaper paste.)

While the pasta is cooking, heat the oil in a deep frying pan over a low-ish hob. Add the garlic, chilli and a pinch of salt, and cook gently – we want the garlic to soften and just begin to change colour so its flavour will be fragrant and nutty, and not harsh.

Add the cooked pasta to the frying pan – this is best done with tongs so a little of the pasta cooking water drips in, which helps to create a beautiful silky kiss of a sauce. Stir well to combine. Add the parsley and give it another quick stir, and add a little salt and pepper to taste. Serve with plenty of grated Parmesan on the side.

ROASTED SWEET PEPPER AND CHILLI RISOTTO

SERVES 2 as a main, or 4 as a starter

3 garlic cloves, peeled and thinly sliced

1 fresh mild to medium red chilli, seeded and sliced

2 tbsp olive oil

2 red peppers, seeded and chopped into 1–2cm (½–¾in) chunks

1 litre (1¾ pints) chicken or vegetable stock

1 tsp soft butter

1 small onion or shallot, peeled and diced

200g (7oz) Arborio or carnaroli rice

125ml (4fl oz) white wine

2 tbsp freshly grated Parmesan cheese

2 tbsp chopped flat-leaf parsley

salt and freshly ground black pepper

Traditionally, chillies are used in the cuisine of southern Italy, while risotto comes from the north. So there's something of a collision of two differing food cultures in this creamy risotto, dotted with sweet and spicy peppers. It is at once comforting and uplifting. Make it on a damp autumn evening when you need a boost, and serve with a glass of robust wine.

First cook the peppers. Soften the garlic and chilli in 1 tablespoon of the olive oil in a large sauté or frying pan over a low heat. As the garlic begins to take on a little colour, add the chunks of pepper. Stir occasionally until the peppers are soft, hot, and a lovely honey-brown. Remove from the heat and set aside.

In a large saucepan, bring the stock to a simmer over a low heat. Keep it on the hob, within easy reach.

Melt the butter with the remaining tablespoon of olive oil in another large saucepan over a low heat. Add the onion. Cook until soft and translucent. Tip in the rice, and stir it in for a couple of minutes, then pour in the wine. Turn up the heat to medium and bubble hard until the rice has absorbed most of the liquid.

Now add a ladleful of stock and cook, stirring the rice, until it has absorbed most of the stock, then add more, repeating the process until the rice is cooked. This can take up to 20 minutes. Note that as you get towards the end of the process, you will want to add the stock in smaller quantities so that your risotto is not too sloppy – you want it nice and creamy, with the grains retaining a little bite.

When the rice is cooked, stir in the peppers. Add the Parmesan, parsley and a grinding of black pepper, and stir together. Add salt to taste. Finally, cover the risotto and allow to rest for a few minutes, then serve.

PAD NOR MAI FARANG FAI DAENG

STIR-FRIED ASPARAGUS
with YELLOW BEANS AND CHILLI

SERVES 2, or 4 as a part of a larger meal

6 small garlic cloves, peeled
pinch of salt
1 Thai orange chilli
3 red Thai bird's-eye chillies
3 tbsp yellow bean sauce, rinsed
1 tsp sugar
1 tbsp oyster sauce
1 tbsp vegetable oil
350g (12½oz) asparagus, trimmed, halved lengthways and cut into 4–5cm (1½–2in) pieces (or use Thai morning glory, see intro)

This is adapted from one of my favourite Thai vegetable dishes, *pad pak boong fai daeng*, made with Siamese water convolvulus or Thai morning glory (not to be confused with the Western garden plant, which is poisonous). But I often make it with asparagus, since that's more readily available. *Fai daeng* means 'red fire', and a good Thai cook knows that the secret to this dish is to catch that deep flamed flavour in the sauce. If you want to, substitute the asparagus with 250g (9oz) of Thai morning glory. It will take a little less time to cook, and won't need the extra water during cooking.

In a pestle and mortar, roughly pound the garlic, salt and chillies together. Set aside.

Mix together the yellow bean sauce, sugar, oyster sauce and 2 tablespoons of water. Set aside.

Heat a wok over a high hob and add the oil. Once smoking, throw in the garlic and chilli, and stir-fry until it's fragrant and golden. Add the asparagus and continue stir-frying for a minute or so.

Scrape in the yellow bean, sugar, oyster sauce and water mixture and move everything around the wok until heated through and bubbling. Try and catch a red flame! Keep stirring for 3–4 minutes, adding another 2 tablespoons of water about halfway through, if needed, until the asparagus is cooked but still retains some bite.

Serve at once, with rice, or with the *Gaeng Hang Lay pork curry* (page 75), the Chao Lay Curried Crab (page 72) or the *Talad Pran Green Curry* (page 62).

MINCED PORK AND GREEN BEANS

SERVES 2 as a main course, or 4 as part of a larger meal

250g (9oz) minced pork

1 tsp Szechuan peppercorns, crushed

2 tbsp vegetable oil

150g (5½oz) green beans, topped, tailed and cut in half

2 garlic cloves, peeled and chopped

2 Thai bird's-eye chillies, chopped

2cm (¾in) fresh root ginger, peeled and slivered

3 tbsp soy sauce

3 tbsp rice vinegar

1–2 tbsp chopped pickled Chinese cabbage (optional)

dash of sesame oil

2–3 spring onions, finely chopped

sea salt, to taste

This simple stir-fry is a sterling example of what the Chinese call *mala*, or numbing hot. Its unique flavour is obtained by combining chillies with Szechuan peppercorns, which are also known as flower pepper or *hua jiao*. These are not strictly peppercorns at all (in fact, they come from the prickly ash tree), and they have an extraordinary tingly heat caused by their apparent stimulation of the parts of the brain which respond to touch.

Place the minced pork in a bowl and mix in the sea salt and the Szechuan peppercorns until well combined.

Heat the vegetable oil in a wok until smoking. Add the green beans and stir-fry for about 1 minute until crisp. Take the wok off the heat and remove the beans with a slotted spoon and set aside on kitchen paper to drain.

Reheat the oil, add the garlic, chillies and ginger and stir until they are just taking on colour. Add the minced pork mixture and carry on frying until the meat is cooked and has taken on some colour. Pour in the soy sauce and vinegar, and stir to combine. Add the pickled cabbage, if using, and then re-introduce the green beans to the dish, stirring them in well. Splash in the dash of sesame oil and remove from the heat.

Scatter with the chopped spring onions and serve with rice.

SZECHUAN AUBERGINES

SERVES 2, or 4 as part of a larger meal

600ml (1 pint) vegetable oil, plus an extra 1 tbsp

1 large aubergine, cut into 2×4cm (¾×1½in) pieces, or 4 Asian aubergines, halved lengthways and chopped

175ml (6fl oz) vegetable stock or water

1 tbsp cornflour

4 garlic cloves, peeled and finely chopped

3cm (1½in) fresh root ginger, peeled and finely chopped

1 heaped tsp Szechuan peppercorns, crushed

2 red bird's-eye chillies, sliced, or 2 dried Szechuan/Tien-Tsin/bird's-eye chillies, roughly chopped

2 tbsp Szechuan chilli-bean paste

½ tbsp light soy sauce

1 tbsp balsamic or black rice vinegar

½ tsp sugar

to serve

2 spring onions, green parts only, chopped

small handful of fresh coriander, chopped

1 tbsp toasted sesame seeds

Szechuan cooking has become hugely popular, packing in the fiery, sour, salty and sweet flavours typical of the region. The fire in this dish comes from a combination of Szechuan peppercorns and chilli. It offers a fascinating insight into the chilli's incorporation into regional Chinese spicing.

Heat the 600ml (1 pint) of oil in a wok over a high flame until very hot – make sure that it is stable so that you don't burn yourself accidentally, and use a wok stand if you need to. Gently pop in the aubergine, being careful not to splash yourself. Fry the aubergine until golden. This may take 2–5 minutes depending on how full your wok is. Scoop the aubergine out with a slotted spoon or wire net and place on kitchen paper to drain. Set aside.

Place the water or stock in a medium saucepan and bring to a simmer on a very low heat. You will need to add the stock to the dish while it's hot.

In a small cup or bowl, mix the cornflour with 2 tablespoons of cold water. Set aside.

Heat another tablespoon of oil in the empty and wiped-out wok until it is smoking. Add the garlic, ginger, peppercorns and fresh or dried chillies, and stir-fry. Stir in the chilli-bean paste until well combined, then return the aubergine to the wok and stir to coat. Pour in the hot stock and bring to the boil. Turn the heat right down and simmer for a few minutes until it is giving and tender.

Add the soy sauce, vinegar and sugar, and stir well. Now scrape the cornflour mixture into the wok and cook in for a minute. Serve, sprinkled with the spring onion greens, chopped coriander and toasted sesame seeds.

CALABRIAN SPAGHETTI
with 'NDUJA SAUSAGE

SERVES 4

375g (13oz) dried spaghetti

2 tbsp extra-virgin olive oil

1 shallot, peeled and finely chopped

2 garlic cloves, peeled and finely chopped

125g (4½oz) 'nduja sausage, skinned

juice of ½ lemon

1 tbsp chopped flat-leaf parsley

sea salt and freshly ground black pepper

freshly grated Parmesan or pecorino cheese, to serve

'Nduja is a soft Calabrian pork sausage cured with the local *peperoncino,* or chilli. It's loosely based on the French andouille sausages introduced to the region in the thirteenth century. Of course, the chilli is a later addition, and now a mainstay of Calabrian cuisine. You can find 'Nduja in Italian delis, most big supermarkets and online.

In salted boiling water, cook the spaghetti according to the packet instructions, until done to your liking.

Meanwhile, heat the oil in a small frying pan over a low to medium heat. Add the shallot, and cook until it's soft and translucent, for about 3 minutes or so. Add the garlic, and cook for another minute, until it's fragrant. Break in the sausagemeat – it has a soft texture, so it will squish rather than crumble – and stir it into the shallot and garlic, breaking it down until completely amalgamated into the oil.

Remove the pan from the heat and add the lemon juice and parsley. Taste and add salt if necessary. Drain the pasta, stir it into the sauce and serve at once, with a sprinkling of grated Parmesan and a good grinding of black pepper.

GRILLS, ROASTS
AND BAKES

A CLUTCH OF GRILLED CHICKENS

Almost every country in the chilli-eating world has a fiery marinade for grilled chicken lurking in its repertoire. Here are some of my favourites.

Each recipe makes enough marinade for one whole chicken. The instructions for cooking the chicken itself can be found on page 112.

OMAR'S CHICKEN

2 tbsp olive oil

1 tsp dried throubi or mixed oregano and thyme

1 tsp Aleppo pepper

good grinding of black pepper

good squeeze of fresh lemon juice, to finish

pinch of salt

This recipe is the product of a story told to me years ago, the story of a picnic in a *caravanserai* on the dusty road from Aleppo to Palmyra. Omar, the bus driver, produced a luscious picnic almost out of nowhere. It included a grilled chicken that sounded so extraordinarily delicious I had to try to recreate it for the storyteller. Whenever I make it now, he tells the tale again.

Some people think that throubi is the same thing as a herb called summer savory. Others think it's a distinct hybrid of thyme and oregano. Either way, its aromatic quality lends itself perfectly to this kind of simple grilling.

This should result in a succulent, spicy chicken, packed with the flavours of the Aleppo pepper and the herbs.

In a small bowl, mix the olive oil, throubi and both types of pepper. Taste and add salt if necessary. Once the chicken is cooked (using the method on page 112), finish with a squeeze of lemon juice.

CONTINUED ▶

▶ CONTINUED FROM PREVIOUS PAGE

PIRI-PIRI CHICKEN

1 small onion, peeled and roughly chopped

2–3 garlic cloves, peeled

15–20 fresh African bird's-eye or Thai bird's-eye chillies

grated zest and juice of ½ lemon, plus juice of an extra ½ lemon, to finish

1 tsp paprika

leaves from 2 flat-leaf parsley sprigs

1 bay leaf

2 tsp sherry vinegar

4 tbsp olive oil

salt and freshly ground black pepper

Originating in Mozambique and made famous in Portugal and South Africa, this is hot stuff. You can tone down the chilli if you want to – but, really, why would you? This works perfectly well with dried piri-piri chillies, but the heat isn't quite as aggressively raw as it is with the fresh ones. Aside from the heat, there is also a lovely acidity from the vinegar and the lemon juice. If you can't find piri-piris, you can use Thai bird's-eyes instead.

Put all the ingredients, except the olive oil, salt and pepper, and extra lemon juice, into a food processor and blitz. Then add the salt, pepper and oil, and blitz again until you have a coarse paste. Marinate and cook your chicken as described on page 112. Squeeze the extra lemon juice over the chicken once it's cooked.

MEXICAN POLLO ASADO

3 garlic cloves, peeled and finely chopped

3 tbsp olive oil

juice of 1½ limes

3 jalapeño chillies, seeded and finely chopped

small handful of fresh coriander, chopped

4 tsp dried Mexican oregano (or normal oregano will do)

2 tsp ground cumin

salt and freshly ground black pepper

Here, I've taken the flavours associated with *carne asada* (traditional marinated Mexican beef) – oregano, garlic and zingy jalepeño, with a backdrop of zesty lime – and applied them to chicken. It's delicious.

Put all the ingredients into a food processor, and blitz until smooth. Marinate and cook your chicken as described on page 112.

POLLO AL DIAVOLO

1 tbsp black peppercorns
½ tbsp white peppercorns
½ tbsp crushed dried chilli
grated zest of 1 lemon
½ tbsp French mustard
4–5 tbsp olive oil
1 tbsp chopped flat-leaf parsley

Fiery Italian grilled chicken; this recipe certainly lives up to its name! Black and white peppercorns provide an intense counterpoint to the smoky dried chilli and sharp French mustard.

Grind the peppercorns roughly in a pestle and mortar. Then take 1 tablespoon of the mixture and, in a bowl, combine it with the remaining ingredients, except the parsley. Marinate and cook your chicken as described overleaf. Once the chicken is cooked, garnish with the chopped parsley.

KASHMIRI SPICED GRILLED CHICKEN

small pinch of saffron
1 tbsp vegetable oil
2 garlic cloves, peeled and crushed
1 tbsp Kashmiri *mirch*
2cm (¾in) fresh root ginger, peeled and finely chopped
1 tbsp garam masala
2 tbsp natural yoghurt
juice of ½ lemon
2 tbsp melted butter, for basting

With garam masala, saffron, ginger and Kashmiri *mirch* (or chilli powder), this is a colourful and vibrant marinade which borrows some of the spicing of a *tandoori* chicken and pops it on the barbecue. What can I say? I'm just a grill who can't say no.

First soak the saffron in the oil for at least 15 minutes, ideally an hour, to extract its flavour. Then, in a small bowl, mix it together with all the other ingredients except the butter. Marinate the chicken as described overleaf.

Note that, with this one, the yoghurt is liable to burn over direct heat, so you will need to grill it indirectly – see method overleaf. You will also need 2 tablespoons of melted butter to baste the chicken while it's cooking.

CONTINUED ▶

▶ CONTINUED FROM PREVIOUS PAGE

GRILLED CHICKEN

SERVES 4

1 whole chicken (1.5kg (3½lb))

First, joint the chicken (or ask your butcher to do it). Either spatchcock it (cut out its spine with a pair of poultry shears and flatten the bird out) or joint it into 8 pieces.

Then prepare the marinade of your choice (pages 109–11). When you've made your chosen marinade, cut slashes into your chicken or chicken pieces. Place in a bowl, pour the marinade over the top, and massage it into the bird. Set aside to marinate for a good hour, longer if you have the time.

You can either cook on a barbecue or, if the weather's inclement, on a griddle pan. For a gas barbecue, fire it up to a good medium heat. For charcoal, burn in the coals until they are covered with an even white ash and you can no longer see any flames. You should be able to hold your hand about 15cm (6in) above the grill for 5–7 seconds.

Grill the chicken on both sides, turning occasionally, until cooked through – this will take between 45 minutes and 1 hour, depending on the conditions (wind, etc.). To check the chicken's cooked, stick a skewer into the fattest bit of its flesh – the juices that run out should be clear. Alternatively, stab it with a meat thermometer – it should read 74°C (165°F).

For the Kashmiri-Style Grilled Chicken, you want to prepare your barbecue for indirect cooking. As with the Jerk Pork opposite, shift the hot coals to the sides with suitable tools, place a drip tray in the middle and grill the chicken over the drip tray with the lid over the barbecue. Turn it from time to time, basting with melted butter. You may want to keep a spray bottle of water to hand to douse any flare-ups.

Alternatively, to cook it indoors, pre-heat the oven to 200°C, 400°F, gas mark 6. Heat a dry griddle pan on the hob to a good medium heat, then grill the chicken on the pan for about 5 minutes on each side, to ensure good char-marks on both sides. Then, turn the bird skin-side up and shift the whole griddle pan into the oven. Bake for a further 40–45 minutes until cooked through.

When the chicken's done, allow the meat to rest for 10 minutes or so before serving.

BARBECUED JERK PORK

WEAR GLOVES
FOR THIS ONE

SERVES 8–12

2–2.5kg (4½–5½lb) pork shoulder, skinned and boned

for the marinade (makes about 360ml (12½fl oz)

1½ tsp black peppercorns

1 tbsp allspice berries (or 1½ tsp ground)

4–6 Scotch bonnet chillies, seeded

leaves from 4 large thyme sprigs

6 spring onions, chopped

1 onion, peeled and chopped

2–3 garlic cloves, peeled and chopped

1 tsp grated fresh nutmeg

1½ tsp ground cinnamon

¼ tsp ground cloves

1 tbsp light or dark soft brown sugar

2 tsp salt

1 tbsp overproof or white rum (optional)

100ml vegetable oil

75ml distilled white vinegar

1 tsp liquid hickory smoke (if using oven)

for the smoke

4 good handfuls of hickory, mesquite or pimento wood chips, soaked in water for at least 30 minutes

2 tbsp allspice berries, soaked in water for at least 30 minutes

Jerk is said to have originated with the Maroons, a community of escaped slaves who lived in the mountains of Jamaica in the eighteenth century. Back then, these spices were used as a preservative. Over time, the technique has evolved into a very specific method of barbecue, and has become Jamaica's national dish. And though the spice blend may change according to each different cook, the fiery Scotch bonnet chillies and allspice always remain.

For this recipe, you will need a good kettle barbecue, either gas or charcoal, and a metal smoke box if you have a gas barbecue. Traditional jerk depends on the smoke of green pimento wood, but you can achieve something very close to a true jerk flavour by mixing allspice berries into wood chips. If you use charcoal, you can put the soaked chips and allspice berries straight on to the hot coals. With gas, use the smoke box, following the manufacturer's instructions. If you really can't access a barbecue, a simple oven method is also given which will get you good results.

You will need to marinate the pork for at least 2 hours or overnight, so plan ahead. If you don't fancy pork, the marinade is also enough for 2–3 spatchcocked chickens (cook as described opposite, using the indirect method).

To make the marinade, break the peppercorns and allspice berries roughly in a pestle and mortar. Place in a blender with all the other marinade ingredients, apart from the vinegar and liquid smoke, and blitz. (If you'd prefer a rougher texture, pound everything in a pestle and mortar.) Stir in the vinegar to loosen the mixture.

Cut slashes in the thicker parts of the pork. Put it in a large bowl or tin, pour over the marinade and work it into the meat. Cover and leave to macerate in the fridge for at least 2 hours or overnight.

CONTINUED ▶

CONTINUED FROM PREVIOUS PAGE

About an hour before you light the barbecue, soak the hickory, mesquite or pimento chips and the whole allspice berries in water.

Heat your barbecue to a good medium heat until all the flames are out, and there is white ash on the coals. When it's ready, ease the coals to the sides of the barbecue and lay a drip tray in between them. Then drain the wood chips and allspice berries thoroughly, and add them to the coals. They will start to smoke immediately. Put the marinated pork on to the grill, over the drip tray, and close the lid. Leave to cook for 2 hours. When the time's up, use a meat thermometer to see if it's done – its internal temperature should be about 75°C (167°F).

When it's cooked, allow the pork a good 20–30 minutes to rest before carving. This is great with Grandma Southby's Rice and Peas on page 149 and the Southern Chilli Kale on page 141, or cut into chunks on wax paper and served with an icy cold beer.

To cook this in the oven, mix a teaspoon of liquid smoke into the marinade at the same time as adding the vinegar. Then, when you're ready to cook, pre-heat the oven to 220°C, 425°F, gas mark 7. Place the pork on a metal rack over a large roasting tray. Put it into the oven, then immediately turn down the oven temperature to 160°C, 325°F, gas mark 3, for 3 hours, or until tender. Baste occasionally and cover with foil if it starts to get too dark.

ROASTED SALMON PIBIL
with FRESH RED ONION PICKLE

SERVES 4

500g (1lb 2oz) salmon fillet, in one piece

banana leaf, to serve (optional)

for the pibil marinade

65g (2¼oz) achiote paste

juice of 1 large orange

juice of 1 lime

½ tsp ground cumin

½ tsp dried Mexican oregano (or normal oregano will do)

pinch of ground cinnamon

1 tsp chipotle in adobo sauce

2 garlic cloves, peeled and chopped

salt and freshly ground black pepper

for the fresh pickle

50ml (1¾fl oz) red wine vinegar

large pinch of salt

1 tbsp caster sugar

1 red onion, peeled and very finely sliced

1 red serenade or Fresno chilli, sliced

1 green jalepeño chilli, sliced

small bunch of coriander, roughly chopped

Pibil is a Mayan word for 'buried', and refers to a time when this dish was cooked or 'buried' in a fire pit. Nowadays, it is cooked wrapped in banana leaves over a grill. Traditionally, it's made with pork, but here the recipe has been adapted for salmon, and there is absolutely no digging involved. This dish includes both the well-known and versatile jalepeño (which, when dried, becomes the chipotle) and the Fresno chilli, which is bright red with a medium spice. Hailing from sunny California, it's widely available.

Achiote paste, which is essential to making *pibil*, originates from the Yucatan peninsula of Mexico. It has a beautiful brick-red colour, and consists of achiote seeds, peppercorns, cloves, allspice, habañero chillies and more. It is widely available from Mexican grocery stores or online.

You ideally need a length of banana leaf for this, but if you cannot find any, foil works perfectly well as a substitute.

First make the *pibil* marinade: mix all the marinade ingredients together in a large bowl – note that, sometimes, the achiote comes in 'brick' form, so you may need to mash it up a bit. Coat the fish thoroughly in the marinade, and leave to macerate for a good hour.

Pre-heat the oven to 200°C, 400°F, gas mark 6. Then soften the banana leaf. You can do this by either blanching it briefly in boiling water or by passing it lightly over a flame on your cooker – you will see it soften visibly.

To make the pickle, mix the vinegar, salt and sugar in a small saucepan. Heat gently, stirring until the sugar has dissolved. Pour the warm vinegar mixture over the onion in a small bowl. Leave to cool. Then add the chillies and the coriander, stir to mix, and set aside until needed.

CONTINUED ▶

▷ CONTINUED FROM PREVIOUS PAGE

Remove the salmon from its marinade, leaving as much of the sauce clinging to the fish as possible, and place it on to the banana leaf or foil. You don't want the fish swimming in sauce, but you want a good measure of it there. Close up the parcel with cocktail sticks (or, if using foil, wrap it loosely), and bake in the oven for 15 minutes, or until cooked.

Serve with the pickle, warmed corn tortillas and slices of avocado, or with the Guacamole Mashed Potatoes on page 151.

CHICKEN ENCHILADAS
with LUIS IGLESIAS'S SALSA

SERVES 4–6

800g (1lb 12oz) tinned tomatillos, drained

200g (7oz) tinned chipotles in adobo sauce

handful of fresh coriander, chopped

2 tbsp vegetable oil

8–12 soft corn tortillas

400g (14oz) cooked skinless chicken, shredded

150ml (5fl oz) soured cream or Mexican crema

75g (2½oz) Cheddar cheese, grated

You can make chicken enchiladas with many different sauces, but I am particularly taken with this one, which is spicy, tart and utterly delicious. It was given to me by my friend Luis, who, with his colleague Oscar, imports a whole host of Mexican ingredients to the UK through their company Mextrade.

Pre-heat the oven to 180°C, 350°F, gas mark 4 and lightly oil a 32 × 22cm (13 × 9in) baking dish.

First, make the salsa: put the tomatillos, the chipotles, their sauce and the coriander into a food processor or blender, and blitz them all together until they form a sauce. Add a little water to loosen, if it seems too thick. Then smear one spoon of the salsa over the bottom of the baking dish. Set the rest aside.

Heat the oil in a non-stick frying pan over a low to medium hob, and gently fry the tortillas for a few seconds on each side until they take on a golden colour but remain soft enough to roll. Set aside on kitchen paper to drain any excess oil.

Divide the chicken equally between the tortillas, rolling them up to make chicken 'cigars'.

As you roll them, lay the 'cigars' in the baking dish to create a single tight layer. Pour the salsa evenly over them, top with the soured cream and sprinkle with the grated cheese. Then bake in the oven for 30 minutes and serve.

OVEN-BAKED PULLED PORK

SERVES 8–10

2kg (4½lb) boned and skinned shoulder of pork
1 tbsp liquid hickory smoke
225ml (8fl oz) beer (of your choice)
4 bay leaves, crushed in your hand
Spicy Barbecue Sauce (page 193), to serve

for the dry rub

2 tsp paprika
1 tsp garlic powder
1 tsp onion powder
2 tsp black pepper
2 tsp brown sugar
1 tsp dry English mustard powder
1 tsp ground cumin
½ tsp nutmeg powder or grated fresh nutmeg
1 tsp cayenne pepper
2 tsp salt

Smoky and subtly spicy, pulled pork would traditionally be made on a barbecue. But this oven method is much more convenient in inclement weather. The paprika and cayenne combine with the other spices to give the pork a lovely mellow, Southern glow. In order to gain that unique smoky flavour that typifies a real barbecue, you can use liquid hickory smoke. It's easily available online. Use it sparingly.

Note that the pork needs to marinate overnight, so start preparing this dish a day in advance.

First, trim the pork shoulder. Cut off the excess fat and cut some slashes in the underside of the joint. Put it into a large bowl or roasting tin and pour the liquid smoke over it. Rub the liquid smoke into the flesh, making sure you work it into the cuts.

Now, in a small bowl, mix together the seasonings and spices to make the dry rub. Spoon it on to the pork and rub it in well. Cover with cling film, and leave it overnight in the fridge.

Allow the pork to come to room temperature before cooking. When you're ready to cook, pre-heat the oven to 200°C, 400°F, gas mark 6. Place the pork in a fresh roasting tin, cover it with a tent of foil and bake in the oven for about an hour. Then turn down the oven to 150°C, 300°F, gas mark 2. Briefly open up the foil and add the beer and bay leaves to the roasting tin. Reseal and bake in the oven for a further 3 hours, basting occasionally.

Now turn up the oven again to 210°C, 420°F, gas mark 6½. Remove the pork, baste it thoroughly and return to the oven, uncovered, for another 15 minutes. Finally, remove from the oven, cover once more and leave to rest for 15–20 minutes. Place the rested pork on a platter and pull it into shreds with two forks. Baste with the remaining cooking juices.

Serve hot or cold in bread rolls, liberally bathed in the Spicy Barbecue Sauce on page 193.

IKAN BAKAR

SPICED FISH
GRILLED in BANANA LEAF

SERVES 4

4 snapper, grouper or sea bass fillets, weighing 550–600g (1¼lb–1lb 5oz) in total

6 large Thai long red chillies, cut in half

2 Thai bird's-eye chillies (optional)

1 lemon grass stick, trimmed, bashed and chopped

2 tsp tamarind purée

3 small Asian shallots or 1 large shallot, peeled and chopped

4 garlic cloves, peeled

2cm (¾in) fresh root ginger, peeled and chopped

2cm (¾in) piece of galangal, peeled and chopped

1 tsp turmeric

1 tsp ground white pepper

½ tbsp shrimp paste

2 tbsp vegetable oil

juice of ½ lime

good pinch of sea salt

banana leaf, to serve (optional)

There used to be a home-style Balinese restaurant on a small street in Bangkok where I regularly had this for lunch. Just the anticipation of opening up the crinkled, slightly charred parcel was enough incentive to order it, and it's enough incentive to make it, too. This version is a slight blend of several recipes, but the end result is spicy, redolent of the region and sings with chilli, tamarind, lemon grass and ginger.

If you can, find banana leaf to wrap this in – the flavour really makes a difference. If not, foil will do fine. You can make this dish on the barbecue or in a grill pan. If you are going to cook on the barbecue, make sure you give it plenty of time to burn in to an appropriate cooking temperature. You want to cook over medium coals – you can tell they're ready if you can hold your hand about 15cm (6in) over the grill and keep it there for no more than 5 seconds.

If you're using a banana leaf, soften it either by running it through a lit flame (a gas hob works fine) so that the leaf quickly changes from shiny to dull, or dip it quickly in boiling water, then dry well. Cut out four large squares, each big enough to wrap a fish fillet. Place one fillet on each piece of banana leaf, or foil, if using.

Whiz the rest of the ingredients to a thick paste in a blender or food processor. Divide evenly over the four fillets. Then wrap up the parcels, securing with a cocktail stick or two for the banana leaf.

Place the parcels on the barbecue or on a heated griddle pan and cook for 5–6 minutes per side – you will see the banana leaf charring, but don't worry, it all adds to the flavour.

Pop the parcels on plates and serve, letting each person open their own. Just watch their faces when the gorgeous spicy scent hits them. Serve with the following *Sambal* on the side.

SPICY SAMBAL

6–8 Thai long red chillies or large red chillies, seeded and chopped
4 Thai bird's-eye chillies
1 tbsp shrimp paste
1 tsp sugar (optional)
fresh lime juice, to taste
lime wedges, to serve

Whoosh all the ingredients in a blender, and serve in small dabs with extra wedges of lime on the side.

BEDOUIN LAMB LEG
on SPICED LEMONY ONIONS

SERVES 8

1 tbsp whole coriander seeds

½ tbsp caraway seeds

50ml (1¾fl oz) olive oil

pinch of saffron threads

1 tsp Aleppo pepper

½ tsp ground cinnamon

sea salt and several good twists of black pepper

1 leg of lamb, 1.5–2kg (3½–4½lb) in weight

2 garlic cloves, peeled and sliced

for the spiced lemony onions

3 tbsp olive oil

750g (1lb 10oz) onions, peeled and thinly sliced (5–6 onions)

1 tsp ground cinnamon

1 tsp cumin seeds, toasted and ground

1 tsp coriander seeds, toasted and ground

2 tsp paprika

pinch of sugar

2 tbsp chopped flat-leaf parsley, plus extra for serving

1 tsp fresh picked thyme leaves

½ tsp sumac powder

½–1 preserved lemon, rind only, finely chopped (about 4 tsp)

good grinding of black pepper

pinch of sea salt

This recipe is adapted from a thirteenth-century Syrian text. It's deceptively simple to make, and fills the kitchen with a delightful scent. Souks and the ancient spice routes of the Near and Middle East come to mind.

It features Aleppo pepper, a semi-dried and coarsely ground spice which is relatively mild with a smoky-fruity flavour. Often it's ground with added salt, so be sure to taste yours first and adapt your seasoning accordingly.

You can buy preserved lemons and sumac – a brick-red and tart, citrusy berry, often sold in powdered form – in most good supermarkets or spice shops.

Pre-heat the oven to 230°C, 450°F, gas mark 8.

Over a low hob, gently toast the coriander seeds and the caraway seeds in a small, dry, non-stick frying pan for a few minutes, until you can smell them. Grind them up in a pestle and mortar and pour them into a small pot with the olive oil and a good pinch of sea salt. Add the saffron, the Aleppo pepper, the cinnamon and the black pepper. Stir together, and leave to infuse for at least an hour.

Cut small incisions into the lamb with a paring knife and insert a slice of garlic into each one.

When the oil has infused nicely, stir vigorously, then spoon half the oil and spice mixture over the lamb and rub it into the joint well.

Roast the lamb in the oven for 25 minutes. Then baste the lamb with half the remaining oil and spice mix, and turn down the oven to 160°C, 325°F, gas mark 3.

Roast the lamb for a further 15 minutes per 500g (1lb 2oz), basting with the remaining oil every 20 minutes or so, until cooked. (These timings should give you a joint that is nicely pink.) Remove from the

CONTINUED ▶

▶ CONTINUED FROM PREVIOUS PAGE

oven and leave to rest. You can bubble up any juices left in the pan and serve with the finished lamb.

While the lamb is in the oven, prepare the Spiced Lemony Onions. Heat the olive oil in a large, heavy-based frying pan over a low hob, add the onions and cook them down, stirring frequently, until they are golden, but not completely soft; you want some bite. Now add all the dried spices apart from the sumac, and add salt and black pepper to taste. Also add the sugar. Cook over a gentle heat, stirring and moving the onions around, for 5–10 minutes or until melty and golden.

Remove the onions from the heat and set aside to cool. When they have reached room temperature, add the fresh herbs, the sumac and the preserved lemon rind and stir through gently. Place them on a platter and scatter with the extra chopped parsley.

When the lamb has rested for about 20 minutes or so, place on top of the onions and bring to the table to carve. Serve with flatbreads and vegetables of your choice, and the Simple Harissa on page 192.

CORNMEAL CATFISH
with LOUISIANA SALSA

SERVES 4

for the salsa

1 red pepper, seeded and diced
1 celery stick, diced
8 small tomatoes, seeded and diced
1 red onion, peeled and diced
1 jalapeño chilli, seeded and diced
1 poblano chilli or ½ green pepper, seeded and diced
2 garlic cloves, peeled and chopped
juice of 1 lime
dash of hot chilli sauce
pinch of salt

for the catfish

125g (4½oz) cornmeal
½ tsp dried thyme
½ tsp cayenne pepper
1 tsp paprika
½ tsp garlic powder
4 catfish fillets (or see intro for alternatives), about 175–200g (6–7oz) each
1 egg white, beaten
3 tbsp vegetable oil
salt and freshly ground black pepper

I don't understand why we don't eat more catfish. Maybe some people find their whiskers offputting, but in Thailand and the US South, catfish is king. It has a firm, meaty flesh and a clean, delicious flavour. The salsa is definitely not traditional, but inspired by the growing Latino community that has developed around New Orleans, while including the Cajun 'holy trinity' of bell peppers, onions and celery.

You can substitute the catfish with skinless tilapia, sea bass or monkfish. And remember, in a lot of places, catfish is sometimes sold as cobbler or river cobbler. Whatever fish fillets you use should not be too thick.

First, make the salsa. In a large bowl, mix all the ingredients together. Leave to macerate for 20 minutes or so.

Now mix together the cornmeal, thyme, cayenne, paprika, garlic powder, a pinch of salt and a good grinding of black pepper. Clean and dry the catfish fillets and season them with salt and pepper. Then dredge them first through the beaten egg, followed by the spiced cornmeal.

Heat 2 tablespoons of the oil in a large, heavy-based, non-stick frying pan over a medium hob, and gently pan-fry the catfish fillets – two at a time, saving the final tablespoon of oil for the second batch – for 3–5 minutes a side, depending on their thickness, until they are cooked through and golden brown and crisp on the outside. Drain for a few seconds on a rack over kitchen paper before serving.

Serve with the Louisiana salsa on the side.

GRILLED SARDINES
with MARAS PEPPER AND PINE NUTS

SERVES 4 as a starter, or 2 as a main

4 garlic cloves, peeled and crushed

1 tbsp Maras pepper

5 tbsp good extra-virgin olive oil, plus extra for brushing the fish

2 tbsp finely chopped flat-leaf parsley

8 sardines, cleaned and gutted

2 tbsp pine nuts, toasted

salt and freshly ground black pepper

Ezme (page 145), to serve

Maras pepper is almost interchangeable with Aleppo pepper, except for the fact that it is distinctly Turkish, while Aleppo pepper seems to be used much more widely. They are grown in the same region and in similar micro-climates. So, if you can't find Maras, Aleppo pepper will do very well. That said, the former is earthy and fruity with a bold heat, and adds a delicious Ottoman warmth to the dressing.

A note on sardines: you can cook them on a griddle pan indoors, but you'll need an industrial extractor fan – they really do stink out the house. As ever, the barbecue adds a delicious smoky quality that cannot be beaten.

First, make the dressing. In a small frying pan, mix the garlic and Maras pepper into the olive oil, and heat gently over a low hob until the oil just begins to quiver. You want the garlic and pepper to infuse into the oil, but not to colour. Remove from the heat and set aside to cool for just a minute. Then add 1 tablespoon of the chopped parsley. Set aside until needed.

Heat a griddle pan or a barbecue to a good medium heat. Brush the sardines with extra-virgin olive oil and season them well with salt. Then grill for 2–3 minutes on each side, until the skin is crispy and the flesh cooked through.

When the fish are cooked, lay them on a platter or divide between plates and dress with the olive oil, garlic, Maras pepper and parsley mixture. Season once more with salt and pepper, then scatter the pine nuts and remaining chopped parsley over the top. Serve at once with the Ezme on page 145 or a leafy salad.

DORSET CHILLI AND APPLE CHICKEN

SERVES 4

3 tbsp olive oil

1 onion, peeled and finely chopped

3 garlic cloves, peeled and finely chopped

1–2 Trinity chillies or ½–1 Scotch bonnet chillies, seeded and finely chopped

1 whole chicken (1.5kg (3½lb)), jointed into 8 pieces, or 1 large rabbit, jointed into 6

2 eating apples, peeled, cored and sliced

2 tbsp Somerset cider brandy (optional)

250ml (9fl oz) cider

1 bay leaf

1 thyme sprig

1 marjoram sprig

250ml (9fl oz) chicken stock

50ml (1¾fl oz) double cream

salt and freshly ground black pepper

I created this dish to celebrate the English Trinity chilli, a habanero varietal developed by Sea Spring Seeds in Dorset. It has a deliciously rich fruit which sits very well with this appley sauce, ideally made with local Dorset cider. You can buy the chillies by mail order when they're in season, but if you can't find them, use a Scotch bonnet as a substitute, though beware as it will be hotter! Speaking of substitutions, I originally made this with rabbit; if you're a rabbit fan, it works beautifully.

Pre-heat the oven to 180°C, 350°F, gas mark 4.

Heat a tablespoon of oil in a large, heavy-based, lidded ovenproof pan over a low to medium hob, and cook the onion until it is translucent. Add the garlic and chilli, and cook for a further 2–3 minutes or until fragrant and just beginning to colour. Remove everything from the pan and set aside.

Turn up the heat, add the rest of the oil and brown the chicken or rabbit pieces thoroughly. You'll need to do this in batches, setting aside as you go. Chicken will take longer than rabbit because it has more fat. You want its skin to turn a nice, golden colour, which could take up to 10 minutes per batch.

Then add the apple and cook until it's just beginning to caramelise. Return the meat to the pan. If you are confident you know what you're doing, you should now add the cider brandy and carefully flambé the dish. If you're not, please skip the flambé.

Add the cider, herbs, onions, garlic, chilli and stock – the liquid should not quite cover the meat. Season with salt and pepper, and bring to a simmer. Put the lid on the pan and put it in the oven for about 45 minutes, until the meat is cooked through.

Now remove the meat, set it aside on a warm plate and cover with foil. Reduce the sauce by at least one-third of its volume by bubbling it on the hob. Then stir in the cream. Bring the sauce back to a simmer, taste and adjust the seasoning. Return the meat to the pan, coat it in the sauce and serve. This goes beautifully with boiled new potatoes and steamed greens.

JAMAICAN CHICKEN FRICASSÉE

WEAR GLOVES
FOR THIS ONE

SERVES 4–6

4 garlic cloves, peeled and crushed

2 tsp paprika

2 tsp ground ginger

1 tsp whole allspice berries, ground in a pestle and mortar

3–4 tbsp vegetable oil

4–7 fresh thyme sprigs, to taste

1 whole chicken (1.5–2kg (3½–4½lb)), jointed into 8 pieces

1 large onion, peeled and chopped

125ml (4fl oz) chicken stock

12 whole cherry tomatoes

1 bay leaf

1 red Scotch bonnet chilli

salt and freshly ground black pepper

CHILLI FACT

The Scotch bonnet is named for its apparent resemblance to a Scottish tam-o'-shanter hat. It is a beautiful, bell-shaped fruit, found primarily in Jamaica and Trinidad. It's extremely fiery, measuring up to a whopping 350,000 on the Scoville scale.

A fricassée is a method of cooking meat or poultry in its own sauce, rather than making the sauce at the end of the process, as you might for a sauté. It's a very popular cooking style across the Caribbean. This version evolved in the kitchens of my husband Fred's Jamaican cousins. Some of them dry-rub the chicken in the spices, some of them marinate it in a little oil, and all of them balance their spices a little differently. This recipe collects the family wisdom into one straightforward dish.

As ever in Jamaican cookery, it stars the Scotch bonnet chilli – its treatment here will determine how hot your fricassée turns out. If you leave the chilli whole, with its stalk on, the dish will have hints of the Scotch bonnet's flavour with little of its heat. If you cut it in half and deseed it, you'll find the dish hotter. And if you add the seeds to the dish, you'll find it hotter still. Be warned, don't touch your eyes or anywhere else that's sensitive until you've washed your hands thoroughly!

In a large bowl, mix together the garlic, paprika, ginger and allspice with 2 tablespoons of the oil. Add a couple of the thyme sprigs and season with salt and pepper. Then rub the mixture into the chicken pieces and leave to marinate for at least 30 minutes, but preferably 3 hours plus. You can certainly leave this, covered, overnight.

When you're ready to cook, heat another 1–2 tablespoons of oil in a large sauté pan, with a lid, over a medium hob. Wipe the marinade from the chicken pieces with your hands, reserving as much as possible, and brown the chicken in batches, setting them aside as you go, until all the pieces are golden brown. Then turn down the heat, add the onion and cook gently until soft and translucent.

CONTINUED ▶

CONTINUED FROM PREVIOUS PAGE

Now add any remaining garlic, paprika, ginger and allspice marinade, and cook for a minute or so until you can really smell the spices. Pour in the stock and bubble it up, scraping up any cooking residues from the bottom of the pan.

Return the chicken to the pan and add the tomatoes, bay leaf and Scotch bonnet (see intro). Bring the fricassée to a simmer and cook gently, covered, for about 45 minutes until the chicken is done.

Remove the chicken from the pan and set aside. Then, over a high heat, reduce the juices by half. Discard the Scotch bonnet, pour the juices over the chicken, and serve with Grandma Southby's Rice and Peas on page 149 and sautéed greens.

XINJIANG-STYLE SLOW-ROASTED SHOULDER OF LAMB

SERVES 6–8

2–2.25kg (4½–5lb) shoulder of lamb

2 green peppers, seeded and sliced into strips

2 onions, peeled, halved and sliced

for the marinade

2 tbsp cumin seeds, toasted

1 tsp Szechuan peppercorns

1 tsp fennel seeds

3 garlic cloves, peeled and roughly chopped

2 tsp ground cumin

3 tsp chilli flakes

3 tbsp vegetable oil

3 tbsp light soy sauce

3 tbsp dry sherry or Chinese rice wine

I've taken inspiration from the famous Xinjiang-style kebabs – skewered lamb grilled over charcoal and flavoured with chilli, Szechuan peppercorns and cumin – where the key is to place big chunks of lamb fat between the meat cubes to baste them as they cook. So, keeping that in mind, shoulder makes the ideal cut for an up-scaled adaptation for feasting.

Note that this dish uses both freshly toasted cumin seeds *and* ground cumin. This broadens the flavour spectrum, and toasting replicates some aspects of the smokiness you'd find in the original grilled kebabs.

Place the lamb in a large roasting tin. Cut several slashes in the flesh with a sharp knife.

In a pestle and mortar, roughly grind the toasted cumin seeds, Szechuan peppercorns, fennel seeds and garlic to form a paste. Add the ground cumin and chilli flakes and stir to combine. Add the vegetable oil, soy sauce, sherry or Chinese rice wine and mix well. Smother the marinade all over the lamb, getting it well into the slashes. Cover and chill for at least 1 hour, but 3–4 hours if possible.

Allow the lamb to come to room temperature and pre-heat the oven to 170°C, 340°F, gas mark 3½.

Pop the lamb, uncovered, in the oven for 15 minutes. Then add 50ml (1¾fl oz) of water to the roasting tin and cover with foil. Cook for 3½–4 hours, or until very tender and falling off the bone. Remove the foil, add the green peppers and onions to the tin and cook in the oven for another 15–20 minutes, or until the vegetables are just cooked through. Remove from the oven and place the lamb on a warm serving dish, surrounded by the peppers and onions.

Skim any excess fat off the remaining juices in the tin and discard. Heat the cooking liquid, and spoon it alongside the lamb. Serve with rice and the vegetables of your choice.

VEGETABLES, SNACKS AND SIDES

FRESH COURGETTE
with CHILLI VINAIGRETTE

SERVES 4 as a side

2 tbsp extra-virgin olive oil

3 tbsp white wine vinegar

pinch of paprika

2 courgettes, topped and tailed, and shaved into ribbons

2 pickled chillies, sliced

½ green bird's-eye chilli, sliced

½ mild Thai long red chilli, sliced

2 spring onions, finely sliced

leaves from 1 fresh thyme sprig

salt and freshly ground black pepper

Thin strips of courgette are quickly pickled in a lightly spiced vinegar – a perfect foil for richer dishes, such as crab cakes, lamb or duck, because its acidity cuts through the fat and refreshes the palate.

In a small bowl, mix the olive oil and white wine vinegar. Add the salt, pepper and paprika. Taste to adjust the seasoning.

Place the courgettes into a large serving dish and pour over the dressing. Mix together gently with your hands along with the chillies, the spring onion and the thyme leaves. Season with a little extra salt and pepper and serve at once.

TIP

If you have a mandolin, use that to shave lovely thin slices of courgette; if not, a potato peeler works fine.

SPICED GREEN BEANS
with CHILLIES AND COCONUT

SERVES 4 as a side

2 tbsp vegetable oil

½ tsp yellow mustard seeds

1 small onion, peeled and finely sliced

1–2 *hari mirch*, or green finger chillies, sliced on the diagonal

200g (7oz) green beans, topped and tailed

1 tsp turmeric

salt, to taste

1 tbsp shredded coconut, to garnish

The vibrant verdure of these beans and the yellow of the turmeric create an explosion of colour on your plate, in much the same way as the mustard and chilli create an explosion of flavour on your palate. Serve as a side with any Indian curry or grilled meat. See photo on page 97.

Heat the vegetable oil in a frying pan over a high heat until it's smoking. Throw in the mustard seeds and cook until they pop. Then add the onions and fry until they are just cooked – a few minutes, no more.

Add the chilli, green beans, turmeric and salt. Mix everything thoroughly until hot all the way through but still crisp, and serve, garnished with the shredded coconut.

SOUTHERN CHILLI KALE

SERVES 4 as a side

75g (2½oz) bacon or bacon lardons, chopped into very small pieces

dash of vegetable oil

2 garlic cloves, peeled and thinly sliced

1 serrano chilli, thinly sliced on the diagonal

large bunch of kale, de-stemmed and roughly sliced (200–250g (7–9oz) prepared weight)

1 tsp white wine vinegar

salt and freshly ground black pepper

This is a lighter, quicker version of southern collard greens, but using kale instead. Kale has a similar bitterness to collard greens, while the bacon gives a porky depth and the serrano chilli adds a punch of heat. If you cannot find kale you could substitute chard or spring greens.

Instead of the serrano chilli, you can use a couple of good pinches of dried chilli, or even a few dashes of your favourite hot sauce – Tabasco, Tapatio, Crystal, Grace are all terrific. If you *do* use hot sauce, leave out the vinegar. Alternatively, you could use a Pickled Chilli (page 207) and a dash of its vinegar.

In a large, dry sauté pan with a lid, cook the bacon lardons over a medium heat until they're golden and crispy. Remove the bacon from the pan with a slotted spoon and set aside on kitchen paper. If the pan's looking a little dry, add a dash of vegetable oil. Then add the garlic and the chilli and sauté until the garlic just begins to colour.

Now add the greens, a handful at a time, tossing them together with the chilli and garlic. When they're all in the pan, season with salt and pepper and the vinegar. Stir until well combined but still bright and green. Reintroduce the bacon and give it one last stir.

Serve with grilled or roasted meats or fish.

CAPONATA SIRACUSA

SERVES 6–8

6–8 tbsp olive oil

2 firm, medium aubergines, cut into 2.5cm (1in) dice

1 red onion, peeled and roughly chopped

2 red or orange Romano peppers, seeded and chopped

1–2 Italian hot red chillies, seeded and chopped

4 celery sticks, chopped

160g (5½oz) cherry tomatoes (about 18), halved, plus 4 more, halved, to garnish

2 tbsp capers, drained

4 tbsp raisins or sultanas, or both

1 tbsp sugar

6–8 tbsp red wine vinegar

handful of flat-leaf parsley, chopped

15 pitted black olives, halved

sea salt and freshly ground black pepper

to serve

1 tbsp extra-virgin olive oil

2 tbsp pine nuts, toasted

toast or crusty bread

This colourful *agrodolce* vegetable medley was always one of the first things I ordered when my family used to sail to Sicily when I was a girl. It's great as a snack on bread or toast, as part of an antipasti platter, or as a side for meat or fish. And it stars the Romano pepper, which is closely related to the bell or sweet pepper. This recipe makes a fairly large amount, but it keeps well and it will disappear in no time.

Heat 2 tablespoons of the olive oil in a heavy-based, lidded pan over a medium hob. You won't need all the oil up front, just add it as you need it.

Add the aubergines – you may have to do this in batches, as you don't want to crowd the pan and cause the aubergines to 'sweat'. You want them a nice goldeny brown on the cut sides. This should take 5–6 minutes. Remove and set aside on kitchen paper.

Heat the final tablespoon of oil in the empty pan and add the onion. Allow it to colour a little. Add the peppers, chilli and celery, and stir well, coating all the vegetables in olive oil. Add the tomatoes and cooked aubergine and stir through, then add the capers and raisins or sultanas. Mix the sugar and vinegar together in a small bowl and add that to the pan too. Cover the pan with a lid and simmer gently for 5–10 minutes, then cook for another 5 minutes uncovered. Add salt and pepper to taste.

Take off the heat and set aside to cool to room temperature. When it's cooled, add the parsley, olives and extra cherry tomato halves and stir through gently. Serve on small plates, drizzle over the extra-virgin olive oil, scatter with the toasted pine nuts and enjoy with toast or crusty bread.

BRAISED ARTICHOKES
with PRESERVED LEMON, CHILLI AND POTATOES

SERVES 4, or 6 as a side

5–6 small violet artichokes

juice of 2 lemons

1 small to medium onion, peeled and sliced

150ml (5fl oz) olive oil

4 garlic cloves, peeled and chopped

small bunch of fresh thyme

2 tsp dried *piment d'Espelette* powder

300ml (10½fl oz) white wine

6–8 new potatoes

1 small preserved lemon, rind only, chopped – about 1½ tsp in all

salt and freshly ground black pepper

4–6 strips preserved lemon peel, to garnish

1 tbsp chopped flat-leaf parsley, to garnish

Picture a French market stall with row after row of beautiful purple-tipped young artichokes tied up like eccentric bridal bouquets: elegantly coloured, stunningly shaped and utterly delicious. And, unlike the bigger artichokes, you can generally eat the whole thing.

An excellent side for char-grilled lamb or a simple light supper on its own, this is a Provençal classic. I've added the *piment d'Espelette*, south-western France's famous chilli (available from specialist grocers or online); it gives the dish a gentle warmth. But if you cannot find it, Spanish paprika makes a good alternative.

Trim the artichokes and cut them in half, removing any choke. Rub the cut halves with a little of the lemon juice to prevent discolouration. Set aside.

In a large, lidded, heavy-based frying pan over a medium hob, sweat the onions in the olive oil until soft. Add the garlic and stir through. Add the artichokes, thyme, *piment d'Espelette*, the juice of one of the lemons, half the wine and 150ml (5fl oz) of water. Cover and simmer for 30 minutes.

Now add the potatoes, the rest of the wine plus another 150ml (5fl oz) of water, the preserved lemon peel, salt and pepper to taste and the juice of the other lemon. Bring to the boil, cover and simmer for 15 minutes, or until the potatoes are just cooked.

Serve the artichokes surrounded by the sauce, each portion toppped with a strip of preserved lemon peel and a scattering of chopped parsley.

EZME

SERVES 4–6 as a side

4 medium tomatoes, seeded and very finely chopped

1 red pepper, seeded and very finely chopped

1 small onion, peeled and very finely chopped

2 garlic cloves, peeled and very finely chopped

½ cucumber, seeded and very finely chopped

1 tbsp tomato purée

2 fresh cayenne or other hot red chillies, seeded and very finely chopped

1 tbsp Maras pepper

1 tbsp finely chopped fresh mint

small handful of flat-leaf parsley, very finely chopped

1 tsp pomegranate syrup (optional)

3 tbsp olive oil

juice of ½ lemon

salt

There are so many versions of this vibrant, sunny Turkish salad (shown on page 129), but two things they all have in common are juicy, ripe tomatoes and chillies. It's the perfect side for grills and roasts, such as Omar's Chicken on page 109 and the Grilled Sardines on page 128, or as part of a mezze platter with fresh flatbreads and olives.

Get all your chopping done, then combine all the ingredients in a large bowl and mix well. Allow to sit for an hour or so before serving so that the flavours can really come together. And that's it.

This keeps for up to a week in the fridge, but becomes more like a dip or salsa in consistency.

ALEPPO PEPPERED BROCCOLI

SERVES 4 as a side

100g (3½oz) breadcrumbs
1 tbsp Aleppo pepper
zest of ½ lemon, finely chopped
2 tbsp olive oil
25g (1oz) butter
400g (14oz) broccoli, trimmed into
florets then sliced lengthways
salt and freshly ground black pepper

This crunchy spiced broccoli with exciting shocks of heat goes brilliantly with roasted lamb or grilled chicken. This recipe makes more of the peppered breadcrumbs than you need, but they keep for up to a week in a sealed container, and go brilliantly sprinkled over all kinds of vegetables, or even ice cream.

Pre-heat the oven to 200°C, 400°F, gas mark 6. In a large bowl, mix together the breadcrumbs, Aleppo pepper, lemon zest, salt and pepper.

In a frying pan, heat 1 tablespoon of the olive oil and the butter over a medium hob. Add the breadcrumb mixture and stir, frying gently, until golden and crispy. Set aside to cool on kitchen paper.

In another bowl, coat the broccoli in the remaining olive oil with your hands and season with salt and pepper. Place on an oven tray, cut-side up, and roast for 10–15 minutes until lightly cooked. Now press the crumbs on to the broccoli and cook for another 2–3 minutes. Remove from the oven and serve.

INDIAN-STYLE ROASTED CAULIFLOWER

SERVES 4–6 as a side

1 tsp coriander seeds

½ tsp yellow mustard seeds

½ tsp black mustard seeds

1 firm cauliflower head, trimmed and broken into florets

3–4 garlic cloves, smashed in their skins

1 *hari mirch* green finger chilli, sliced on the diagonal

3 tbsp vegetable oil

salt and freshly ground black pepper

Crisp cauliflower roasted with aromatic spices and the punchy Indian *hari mirch* or green finger chilli; this makes a great side dish to grilled or roasted meats, as shown on page 96, or also goes nicely with Indian curries.

Pre-heat the oven to 180°C, 350°F, gas mark 4. In a pestle and mortar, roughly crack the coriander and both types of mustard seeds. Mix well with the rest of the ingredients in a large bowl.

Turn everything out into a roasting tin, and bake in the oven for 15 minutes. Then turn the oven up to 200°C, 400°F, gas mark 6, and bake for another 5–7 minutes, until the cauliflower turns brown and crispy at the edges. Serve at once.

GRANDMA SOUTHBY'S RICE ⊞ PEAS

SERVES 4 as a side

1 tbsp vegetable oil
25g (1oz) butter
1 onion or 3 spring onions, peeled and chopped
100g (3½oz) smoked bacon lardons
1 garlic clove, peeled and chopped
200g (7oz) long-grain rice
3–4 thyme sprigs
200ml (7fl oz) chicken stock or water
200ml (7fl oz) coconut milk
400g tin of red kidney beans, drained and rinsed
1 Scotch bonnet, left whole
salt and freshly ground black pepper

This kidney-bean-studded, coconut-infused rice dish is a Jamaican classic and one of those recipes that provokes debate. Jamaican home cooks each have a different version, and will insist that theirs is the only one that's 'right'. This version is based on a recipe from my husband's grandma, who was Montego Bay born and bred. She used a smoked pork hock or knuckle, but I use bacon lardons for speed. They add a glorious smoky richness to the dish. The whole Scotch bonnet makes it properly Jamaican and gives the rice and peas a soft warmth. If you prefer something spicier, seed and chop the Scotch bonnet and add it at the same time as the garlic. But, if you're chopping the Scotch bonnet, remember to wear gloves!

Serve as a side with the Barbecued Jerk Pork on page 113 or any grill or barbecue.

In a large lidded saucepan, melt the oil and butter over a medium hob, add the onion or spring onions and bacon, and cook for a few minutes until the onion is translucent and the bacon begins to take on some colour.

Add the garlic and cook for a couple of minutes longer – just until you can really smell it.

Now add the rice and the thyme. Stir together so that the rice is evenly coated with the fats. Then add the stock or water, the coconut milk, the beans and the whole Scotch bonnet.

Season with salt and pepper and bring to the boil; then cover with the lid, turn down the heat and simmer for 12–15 minutes, until cooked to your liking.

Taste and adjust the seasoning. Then cover again, remove from the heat and leave to rest for 5 minutes or so, discarding the Scotch bonnet before serving.

JOLLOF RICE

WEAR GLOVES
FOR THIS ONE

SERVES 4 as a side

250g (9oz) long-grain or basmati rice

3 tbsp peanut or vegetable oil

1 onion, peeled and chopped

2 garlic cloves, peeled and chopped

1 habanero or Scotch bonnet chilli, seeded and chopped

leaves from 4 thyme sprigs

1 bay leaf

2 tbsp tomato paste

1 tsp curry powder

2 tsp paprika

1 tsp cayenne pepper

½ tsp ground ginger

500ml (18fl oz) vegetable stock

sea salt and freshly ground black pepper

Many say that Jollof Rice is the origin of New Orleans Jambalaya. It's a West African staple; no party is complete without a big bowl of *jollof* or 'one pot' rice – sometimes on the side, sometimes cooked with chicken. Nigerians, Ghanaians and Gambians of my acquaintance have all claimed theirs is the best. So, in order to be fair, here is a simple version of my own, which goes very well with grills and roasts.

West African food is often highly spiced and features those New World imports, the tomato and chilli. Once again, the chillies travelled with the Portuguese, but they took so well to the West African climate that they broke loose from their domesticity and are now found wild across the region.

In a sieve, rinse the rice a few times under cold running water, then drain and set aside.

Heat the peanut oil over a medium hob in a large, heavy-based lidded pan. Fry the onion until soft. Add the garlic and Scotch bonnet and fry for another minute, then add the rice and coat it well.

Add the thyme, bay leaf, tomato paste, curry powder, paprika, cayenne pepper, ginger and salt and pepper, then pour in the stock and bring to the boil. Then turn down the heat, cover and simmer for about 20 minutes, or until the liquid has been absorbed and the rice is cooked (it should be just soft). Turn off the heat and allow the rice to rest for a good 10 minutes before serving. Season to taste.

GUACAMOLE MASHED POTATOES

SERVES 4 as a side

4 medium-sized potatoes, peeled and cut into chunks

1 ripe avocado

2–4 tbsp olive oil, plus an extra drizzle for serving

2 spring onions, including green parts, finely chopped

handful of fresh coriander, finely chopped

1 jalepeño or serrano chilli, seeded and finely chopped

salt and freshly ground black pepper

I love guacamole; I love mashed potatoes. If ever there were a dish to symbolise the way my mind works, this is it. It's mildly spicy, thanks to the jalepeño, and bears a creaminess that only avocado can bring. This goes beautifully with the Roasted Salmon Pibil on page 117 or any grilled or roasted meat or fowl your heart desires.

For a deeper flavour, blister the peppers over a gas flame for a few minutes, then chop them into the mash.

Boil the potatoes in salted water until cooked through, then strain and mash. Add the avocado flesh and olive oil, and mash them into the potato thoroughly. Stir in the spring onion, coriander and chilli, season with salt and pepper, add an extra drizzle of olive oil, and serve.

SPICED POLENTA

SERVES 4 as a side

60g (2oz) unsalted butter, plus extra
for greasing and frying

150g (5½oz) fine polenta svelte
(quick-cook polenta)

25–30g (1oz) Parmesan, grated

1 jalapeño chilli, finely chopped (see
intro for advice on seeding)

½ tsp ground cumin

1 tbsp chopped coriander

1–2 tbsp extra-virgin olive oil

a little regular olive oil, for frying

salt and freshly ground black pepper

TIP

For a change, you might like to roast
the jalepeño. Hold it with tongs over
a gas flame for a few minutes to char
it. Then put it into a plastic bag for
another 10 minutes to steam, which
will allow you to peel it more easily.
Peel and chop before making the
polenta and add it in place of the raw
jalepeño. This gives the polenta a
deeper, smokier flavour.

This recipe gives the chillies and corn of Mexican cuisine
an Italian twist. The heat of the jalepeño and the warmth of
the cumin work magically with the cheesy-creamy polenta.

Before you make this, taste a tiny piece of your jalepeño.
Sometimes they can be very mild, in which case you might
want to retain the seeds for extra heat. Or, if it's one of the
hot ones, you might prefer to deseed it, to dial it down.

Heat 750ml (1¼ pints) of salted water in a large saucepan over a
medium–high hob.

When it has come to a rolling boil, add the polenta, turn down
the heat and stir until it starts to thicken. How long this takes will
depend on the polenta you are using. If it is svelte, or quick-cook,
this should only take about 8 minutes, but check the packaging.

Remove the saucepan from the heat and add the butter, grated
cheese, chilli, cumin and chopped coriander. Stir everything in well,
season with salt and pepper and add the extra-virgin olive oil. Stir
again and serve immediately.

Alternatively, you can pour it into a greased baking dish and let
it go completely cold. Once cold, cut the polenta into squares or
triangles. Then either fry the pieces gently in olive oil and butter,
or oil each piece and cook it on a griddle pan over a medium heat.
It should take a couple of minutes on each side. In the frying pan,
you want it to turn nicely golden on both sides; on the grill, you're
looking for good char lines to add a crispy finish.

CORNBREAD
with CHEESE AND CHILLIES

SERVES 12 as a side

a little butter, for greasing

125g (4½oz) cornmeal

110g (4oz) plain flour

1 tbsp sugar

1 tsp sea salt

1 heaped tbsp baking powder

65ml (2¼fl oz) vegetable oil or melted butter

100ml (3½fl oz) milk

100ml (3½fl oz) buttermilk

1 large egg, lightly beaten

1 jalapeño or serrano chilli, seeded and finely chopped

25g (1oz) sharp Cheddar cheese, grated

This moist and moreish cornbread (see photo on page 57) gets an extra Tex-Mex kick from the chillies. Serve on the side of stews and barbecued meats. It's delicious smeared with one of the flavoured butters on page 213. Make sure the butter is slightly softened so it can melt into the delicate cornbread.

Pre-heat the oven to 200°C, 400°F, gas mark 6. Grease a 20cm (8in) square baking tin with butter.

Combine the dry ingredients in a large bowl. Then add the wet, mixing together thoroughly until you have a soft, dropping consistency – you may need to add a little more milk or buttermilk to achieve this. Stir in the chilli and the cheese, mix thoroughly and pour into the prepared tin.

Bake in the oven for 20–25 minutes, until golden. To test that it's cooked, jab it in its thickest part with a cocktail stick or skewer. If the stick comes out clean, it's done. If not, pop it back in the oven for a few minutes and then test again. Leave to cool in the tin for a few minutes before serving warm.

STUFFED POBLANO PEPPERS

SERVES 4–6

4–6 poblano or Anaheim chillies, with stems attached

150g (5½oz) Cheddar cheese, grated

zest of ½ lemon

good pinch of dried Mexican oregano (or normal oregano will do)

225ml (8fl oz) vegetable oil, for frying

sea salt and freshly ground black pepper

Mexican Roasted Tomato Sauce (page 210), to serve

for the batter

4 tbsp plain flour

4 large eggs, separated (cold eggs work better for this)

salt and freshy ground black pepper

Relleno means 'stuffed', so this is one of those recipes where what you see is exactly what you get. In this case, it's a glossy green poblano chilli stuffed with cheese and fried in a light batter. Poblanos are generally fairly large, so one is enough for each serving. They come from the region of Puebla in Mexico, so this is very much a signature dish. When they're green, poblanos are very mild, measuring between 500 and 1,500 on the Scoville scale. But, like the Padrón pepper, sometimes you'll find an unsuspected firecracker lurking among them.

Once you've mastered the basic battering and frying, you can play around with the stuffing ingredients to make this recipe your own. The finished peppers are great served with the Mexican Roasted Tomato Sauce on page 210.

Over a gas flame, blister the chillies until they are blackened on all sides – be careful! (If your hob is electric, you can do this under the grill or in a griddle pan instead.) Once blackened, pop them into a plastic bag, or into a bowl covered with cling film, and leave for 10–15 minutes; the steam will help loosen the skin. Then peel them carefully. With a very sharp knife, make a small slit in one side of the chilli and gently scrape out the seeds and membrane with a teaspoon or a small spatula. Set aside.

Mix the cheese, lemon zest and oregano together and season with salt and pepper to taste. Gently stuff the peppers with the cheese mixture. You want them full but not overfull – the seams of the peppers need to come together to keep the filling intact when frying. If you are worried, just carefully secure the two sides together with a cocktail stick – but don't forget it's there when you serve them. Now place the peppers in the fridge for 30 minutes.

Just before you are ready to fry the *chiles rellenos*, sort out your

CONTINUED ▶

▶ CONTINUED FROM PREVIOUS PAGE

prep area. You want to be able to move quite quickly, as the batter will collapse if left standing too long.

Place 3 tablespoons of the flour in a wide, shallow bowl and season well with salt and pepper. Now, in a very clean large bowl, whisk together the egg whites until they form stiff peaks. Beat in the remaining tablespoon of flour. Then beat in the egg yolks, one by one, until incorporated and you have a light, fluffy batter.

Remove the *chiles* from the fridge. Place the oil in a wide non-stick frying pan or skillet. It should be about 2cm (¾in) deep. Heat the oil over a medium flame until it's hot – test a drop of batter to see if it sizzles and turns golden. Then, holding the *chiles* by their stems, dredge them lightly in the seasoned flour, shaking off any excess, and dip them into the batter so that they are completely covered. Pop them into the hot oil and fry gently, turning them by using their stems, or very gently with a spatula and tongs, until they are golden brown all over – 1–2 minutes a side should do it. You can 'baste' the sides if they are very large by gently (and carefully) spooning hot oil over them.

Remove with tongs and set on kitchen paper to drain. Serve hot with the roasted tomato sauce.

PIPERADE

SERVES 2 on its own, or 4 with Bayone ham or bacon

6 large eggs, lightly beaten

1 tsp *piment d'Espelette* powder

2 tbsp olive oil

1 small onion, peeled and chopped

2 garlic cloves, peeled and chopped

2 tomatoes, chopped

1 red pepper, seeded and cut into strips

1 green pepper, seeded and cut into strips

1 tbsp chopped flat-leaf parsley, plus extra to serve

sea salt and freshly ground black pepper

The Sunday papers, a pot of fresh coffee, a plate of piperade – it's the perfect brunch! Piperade is a classic French egg dish, packed with the flavours of the French Basque country – garlic, sweet peppers and the region's signature chilli, *piment d'Espelette*, which imbues a dish with the warmth of autumn sunshine.

This dish is traditionally served with slices of Bayonne ham gently fried in olive oil or goose fat, but it's also great with bacon at breakfast, or with salad and a glass of wine as a stand-alone meal.

Season the beaten eggs with the *piment d'Espelette* and a little salt and pepper. Set aside.

Heat the olive oil in a medium frying pan or sauté pan over a medium hob. Add the onion and cook gently for a few minutes, until it begins to soften. Add the garlic and cook a few seconds, then add the tomatoes and the peppers. Season with a pinch of salt and mix well. Now add the eggs and cook gently, stirring all the time – you want a soft, creamy amalgamation. Just as they are setting, take the pan off the heat, add the parsley and carry on stirring, until you have the texture you want.

Serve immediately, scattered with extra chopped parsley.

CHILLI FACT

The *piment d'Espelette* chilli comes from the area around the village of Espelette in the foothills of the Pyrenees. There, they hold an annual festival in its honour in late October. It can be used fresh or dried, but it's generally sold powdered. It's not too hot, clocking in between 2,000 and 4,500 on Professor Scoville's scale. If you can't find it, you can substitute paprika, but that lacks the Espelette's fruit-meets-hay aroma as well as its soft warmth.

MASALA OMELETTE

SERVES 1

1 small shallot, finely chopped (about 25g (1oz) in total)

1 Indian green finger chilli, finely chopped

2 tbsp finely chopped fresh coriander, plus an extra sprig to garnish

½ tsp turmeric

½ tsp garam masala

¼ tsp Kashmiri *mirch*

3 eggs

1 tbsp vegetable oil

squeeze of fresh lemon juice

salt and freshly ground black pepper

Eggs embrace chilli like an old friend, creating a plate of food that's soothing and feisty by turns. This spicy omelette features Kashmiri *mirch*, a powder made from red chillies grown in the Kashmir region of India and Pakistan. It has a mellow heat and a sweet, warm flavour. And it's readily available from most good stockists or on the internet. If you can't find it, you can substitute it with chilli powder, but it's well worth making the effort to source the real thing.

In a small bowl, mix together the shallot, chilli, salt, pepper, coriander and spices. Then gently whisk in the eggs.

Heat the oil in a non-stick frying pan over a medium hob, then pour in the egg mixture. Distribute it evenly across the pan, and cook for 2–3 minutes, until the bottom has set. Flip the omelette and cook for a further minute or so. Turn out on to a plate, and squeeze over the lemon juice, garnishing with a coriander leaf. Have it for breakfast, or serve for lunch with a salad and bread or chapatti.

DESSERTS AND DRINKS

CHILLI KEY LIME PIE

SERVES 8

150g (5½oz) butter, melted, plus extra for greasing

350g (12½oz) digestive biscuits

1 heaped tsp cayenne pepper

3 egg yolks

grated zest of 2 limes

400ml tin of sweetened condensed milk

juice of 6 limes (about 150ml (5fl oz))

2 green jalapeño chillies, seeded and very finely chopped

to serve

300ml (10½fl oz) double cream, whipped

extra grated lime zest

sprinkling of cayenne pepper or chilli powder

Here, the classic key lime pie is given a little heat thanks to the jalapeño chillies. Key limes are small green limes with a sharp citrus bite. They come from Florida where, unfortunately for the rest of us, they have a very short season – so if you can find them, lucky you! The rest of us will have to make do with regular limes. For an extra rich custard, try replacing the egg yolks with duck egg yolks, and if you really want to give this a kick, use seeded green bird's-eye chillies in place of the jalapeños.

Pre-heat the oven to 170°C, 340°F, gas mark 3½. Lightly grease a 23cm (9in) tart tin with a removable base.

Place the biscuits and cayenne or chilli powder in a food processor and blitz into crumbs. Add the melted butter, and pulse until everything is well combined. Tip the crumbs into the tart tin and gently press across the base and up the sides (to a height of about 3cm (1½in)) to mould them into a pie crust. Bake in the oven for 10–15 minutes, or until lightly brown and crisp. Set aside to cool.

Meanwhile, in a large, clean bowl, beat the egg yolks with the lime zest until pale cream in colour and well combined. It should only take a minute or so. Add the condensed milk and the lime juice, and beat again. Then stir in the chillies.

Pour the mixture into the crust and bake for another 15 minutes, or until the filling is just set, but still has a bit of wobble in the middle. Remove and set aside to cool. Once it's cold, put in the fridge for at least 3 hours, or overnight, covered with cling film.

Before serving, remove the pie from the fridge and top with the whipped cream. Sprinkle with the extra lime zest and a dusting of the cayenne or chilli powder. Serve immediately.

PALETAS

Paletas are Mexican frozen treats like popsicles or ice lollies. Originating in Michoacán, they are hugely popular and you can find *paleterías* all over Mexico. Here are three utterly delicious favourites. You will need a good blender, ice-lolly moulds and sticks to make these.

MANGO, CHILLI AND MEZCAL PALETA

MAKES 8–10

100g (3½oz) caster sugar
½ jalapeño chilli
400g (14oz) mango flesh, chopped (approx. 2 large mangoes)
4 tbsp mezcal
1 tbsp fresh lime juice
1 tbsp tamarind purée
juice of 1 large orange (about 3 tbsp)
2 tsp chilli flakes
pinch of salt

Lush mangoes, fruity jalapeño chillies and a shot of mezcal, tequila's older brother, makes this a refreshing but very grown-up treat.

First make some sugar syrup: place 240ml (8½fl oz) of water in a saucepan with the sugar and halved jalapeño and bring to the boil over a medium heat. Then turn down the heat and simmer for 5 minutes. Remove from the heat and set aside to cool. Once cool, strain through a sieve and set aside. Discard the jalapeño.

Place all the remaining ingredients in a blender with the sugar syrup and whoosh. Taste and add more chilli flakes, if you like. Pour evenly into the ice-lolly moulds, not forgetting the sticks, and freeze for at least 6 hours, or until needed.

CONTINUED ▶

▶ CONTINUED FROM PREVIOUS PAGE

PEPPERED STRAWBERRY AND COCONUT PALETA

Smooth, creamy coconut meets fiery fruit, combining to make a lolly that's both comforting and provocative.

MAKES 8–10

400ml (14fl oz) coconut milk

200ml (7fl oz) double cream

100g (3½oz) palm sugar

good pinch of sea salt

250g (9oz) strawberries, hulled and quartered or roughly chopped, if very large

1 Fresno or medium red chilli, seeded and chopped

large pinch of cayenne pepper or chilli powder

½ tsp freshly ground black pepper

Gently heat the coconut milk and cream with the palm sugar and salt until the sugar has dissolved. Do not let it boil. Remove from the heat and allow to cool.

Put half the strawberries, the chilli and the cayenne or chilli powder in a blender and whoosh until you have a textured purée.

Divide the remaining strawberry pieces between the lolly moulds (try and get some to stick only halfway down so they're ultimately in the middle of the finished paleta).

Stir the purée into the coconut milk mixture along with the black pepper. Mix well. Pour evenly and gently into the moulds. Put the lolly sticks in place and freeze for at least 6 hours, or until needed.

KICK-ASS LIME PALETA

Zingy and refreshing, this lime, salt and bird's-eye chilli combination is just the thing for hot sticky days.

MAKES 6–8

200g (7oz) caster sugar (but do taste the syrup – you may prefer it sweeter)

grated zest of 2 limes

4 green bird's-eye chillies, chopped

200ml (7fl oz) fresh lime juice (approx. 7–10 limes)

good pinch of sea salt, to taste

Make a sugar syrup by mixing together the sugar, lime zest, chillies and 400ml (14fl oz) of water in a small saucepan, and bringing to the boil over a low heat. Simmer for 2–3 minutes, or until the sugar has dissolved. Set aside to cool, then strain once cold.

Add the lime juice and salt to taste, and freeze in lolly moulds with sticks, as in the previous two recipes.

CREOLE-ISH SPICED PRALINE CHEESECAKE

SERVES 8

for the spiced pralines (makes 20–24)

200g (7oz) pecans
300g (10½oz) light brown sugar
½ tsp ground cinnamon
3 tsp cayenne pepper
large pinch of sea salt
160g (5½oz) unsalted butter
2 tbsp double cream

for the cheesecake

200g (7oz) digestive biscuits
100g (3½oz) ginger nut biscuits
125g (4½oz) butter, melted
300ml (10½fl oz) double cream
500g (1lb 2oz) full-fat cream cheese (ideally Philadelphia)
juice of 1 lemon
150ml (5fl oz) sweetened condensed milk

to serve

ground cinnamon (optional)
cayenne pepper (optional)
whipped cream

I call this 'Creole-ish' because of the cayenne pepper used to spice up the traditional pecan praline that is crumbled into the cheesecake. There's something quite exciting about the way chilli and cream combine; one agitates the palate, the other soothes and cools. This spiced-up, New Orleans version of a classic unbaked cheesecake demonstrates that contrast perfectly. You'll need to begin this two days before serving – the spiced pralines require time to cool, and the cheesecake needs time to set. There'll undoubtedly be some pralines left over, but don't worry – they won't last long! Serve them with coffee after dinner.

First make the pralines. Pre-heat the oven to 180°C, 350°F, gas mark 4. Place the pecans on a baking tray, breaking a handful in half, and toast in the oven for about 5 minutes – be careful not to let them burn. Remove and set aside to cool.

Lay out a couple of sheets of greaseproof paper. In a bowl, thoroughly mix the sugar, cinnamon, cayenne pepper and salt.

Place the spiced sugar mixture into a medium saucepan with the butter, double cream and 4 tablespoons of water, and put over a low–medium heat until dissolved, stirring all the time. Once the butter has melted and the sugar has dissolved, add the pecans.

Bring to the boil and bubble gently for about 10 minutes, monitoring all the time and stirring occasionally. You want to cook until the sugar mixture reaches the 'soft ball' stage – i.e. when you drop a little into cold water, it should form a soft, fudge-like ball. Then remove from the heat and stir briskly with a wooden spoon until the mixture is glossy.

Spoon the mixture on to the greaseproof paper to make individual discs of about 4cm (1½in) across, and leave to cool thoroughly, which may take several hours. When the pralines are completely

CONTINUED ▷

cool, carefully peel them off the paper and store in an airtight container until needed.

To make the cheesecake, pre-heat the oven to 160°C, 325°F, gas mark 3 and butter a 23cm (9in) round, springform cake tin.

Put all the biscuits into a food processor or blender and whoosh until they are finely ground. Pour the melted butter on to the crumbs and pulse until well combined. Press the crumb mixture into the bottom of the tin to form a solid base and pop into the oven for 15–20 minutes, or until golden brown. Remove and set aside to cool completely.

In a large bowl, beat the double cream and cream cheese with an electric whisk until the mixture forms stiff peaks. Beat in the lemon juice and condensed milk until well combined and smooth.

Carefully break up about 175g (6oz) of the pralines into rough pieces, reserving the best-looking ones to decorate the cheesecake at the end, and gently stir the chunks through the cream-cheese mixture – you want to retain some texture. Spoon the mixture on to the cooled biscuit base, smoothing the top with a spatula. Cover with cling film and chill for 8 hours or overnight.

Before serving, decorate with several of the reserved pralines and a dusting of cinnamon and cayenne, if you like. Serve with whipped cream on the side.

APRICOT CRUMBLE
with LAVENDER AND ALEPPO PEPPER

SERVES 4–6

for the filling
butter, for greasing
750g (1lb 10oz) fresh apricots, halved and stoned
1 tsp Aleppo pepper
2 tsp dried herb lavender
1 tbsp caster sugar
juice of ½ lemon

for the crumble
160g (5½oz) unsalted butter, chilled and cubed, plus extra to dot the crumble top
225g (8oz) plain flour
125g (4½oz) demerara sugar
2 tsp Aleppo pepper
2 tbsp ground almonds
pinch of sea salt

Fragrant, sweet and spicy, this dessert just screams of long, hot summers in southern France. The Aleppo pepper combines with the herb lavender – which you can now find packaged specifically for cooking in the spice section of most supermarkets – to create an intriguingly delicious flavour that is oddly not dissimilar to ginger. It's one of those desserts you'll want to save room for. Maybe for seconds, too.

Pre-heat the oven to 200°C, 400°F, gas mark 6 and lightly butter an 18 × 30cm (7 × 12in) baking tin.

Place the apricots in the tin. Sprinkle with the Aleppo pepper, lavender, caster sugar and lemon juice. Mix well to combine.

Now prepare the crumble mixture. In a large bowl, rub the cold butter into the flour until it resembles breadcrumbs – make sure you leave some chunky bits for extra crunch. Stir in the demerara sugar, Aleppo pepper, ground almonds and sea salt. Cover the apricots with the crumble mixture, and dot with a little extra butter if you like.

Bake in the oven for 35–40 minutes, or until golden and crunchy. Serve with cream or ice cream.

TIP
You can make the crumble mix up to a day ahead and store it in the fridge, covered.

ROASTED NECTARINE, CHILLI AND BASIL SORBET

SERVES 4

800g (1lb 12oz) ripe nectarines

210g (7½oz) caster sugar

handful of basil leaves

1 serrano or medium hot chilli, roughly chopped

2 tbsp *shichimi togarashi*, to serve

The chilli gives this summery sorbet a refreshing, zingy lift with it's unexpected but surprisingly gentle heat, so it's the perfect thing to liven you up after a heavy meal. The sorbet also features *shichimi togarashi*, a uniquely Japanese condiment that lends itself to many dishes. It's a blend of seven flavours: chilli pepper, hemp seed, orange peel, sesame, ginger, seaweed and *sancho*, which is sometimes referred to as Japanese pepper. It adds a deep 'umami' flavour to the sorbet that balances the sweetness of the roasted fruit. It's easy to find in most Japanese stores or online. You need an ice-cream machine to make this sorbet.

Pre-heat the oven to 180°C, 350°F, gas mark 4. Wash and halve the nectarines, and remove their stones. Lay them, flesh-side up, on a clean baking tray, and roast in the oven for 20 minutes.

Meanwhile, pour 185ml (6½fl oz) of water into a small saucepan and add the sugar. Rip the basil leaves into the pan and add the chilli. Heat the mixture slowly over a low hob, stirring often, until just coming to the boil. Then remove from the heat and set aside to cool.

When the nectarines are cooked, remove from the oven and set aside. Once they're cool enough to handle, peel off their skins. Strain the sugar syrup into a bowl or container, discarding the basil and chilli. Put the syrup, nectarines and any of their roasting juices into a blender or food processor, and blitz until smooth. Refrigerate until cold.

Churn the sorbet in an ice-cream machine, according to the manufacturer's instructions, then put it in the freezer until you're ready to serve (at least four hours or until firm). Sprinkle each portion with a little *shichimi togarashi* just before serving. If you've made this ahead of time, you might want to remove from the freezer 10–15 minutes before you want to serve it, to allow it to soften a little.

CHILLI AND ROSE BAKLAVA

MAKES 18–24 pieces

200g (7oz) unsalted butter, plus extra for greasing

12 sheets ready-made filo pastry (have a few more on standby, as it dries out quickly)

for the syrup

100ml (3½fl oz) clear honey, plus an extra drizzle to finish

100g caster sugar

2 tbsp rosewater

2 tsp Maras pepper flakes

4 cardamom pods, lightly crushed

2 star anise

for the filling

225g (8oz) light brown sugar

125g (4½oz) shelled walnuts

100g (3½oz) shelled pistachios

100g (3½oz) ground almonds

1 tsp ground cinnamon

1 tsp Maras pepper flakes

seeds from 10 cardamom pods

You'll find baklava – filo pastry layered with nuts and drenched with syrup – all across the Middle East. It may even be one of the oldest prepared sweets on earth. I have updated and chilli-fied this version, based on the one I made for *Leon: Family and Friends*. It's sweet and aromatic with just a hint of spice from the Turkish Maras pepper and the subtle fragrance of roses.

Pre-heat the oven to 180°C, 350°F, gas mark 4 and grease a 30 × 22cm (12 × 8½in) roasting dish with a little butter.

Mix all the syrup ingredients in a pan with 200ml (7fl oz) of water, and put over a gentle hob until the sugar dissolves. Then simmer for 5–8 minutes, until thick and fragrant. Set aside to cool completely.

Place all the filling ingredients in a food processor and blitz until they're broken down into a textured crumb. Set aside.

Gently melt the butter in a small saucepan over a low heat, then remove from the hob. Unroll the filo pastry and cut the sheets in half – the pieces should be about 20 × 30cm (8 × 12in). Keep any sheets that are not in use covered with a damp tea towel.

Working as speedily, yet as carefully, as you can, begin layering the pastry in the roasting dish, a sheet at a time, generously brushing each sheet with melted butter until you have stacked 10 sheets. Now spoon on about one-third of the filling in an even layer that just covers the filo. Place another filo sheet on top, butter again, and repeat with another third of the filling, then another buttered sheet and the remaining filling. Finish with a final ten sheets of filo, buttering as you go, and giving the top sheet a final lick of butter.

Using a very sharp knife, carefully cut the baklava on both diagonals into 18–24 diamond-shaped pieces. Take care to cut all the way through.

CONTINUED ▶

▶ CONTINUED FROM PREVIOUS PAGE

Bake the baklava in the oven for 40–45 minutes. (Check it after 30 minutes, though: you want a golden-brown, crisp exterior.) As soon as the baklava comes out of the oven, pour the cool syrup evenly over the top. Finish with a good drizzle of honey.

Let the baklava go completely cold in the roasting dish before gently removing. The star anise and cardamom pods look beautiful for presentation but pick them off before eating. The baklava will keep in a sealed container for up to a week . . . if they hang around for that long!

CHOCOLATE, ORANGE AND URFA PEPPER POTS

SERVES 6

160g (5½oz) dark chocolate, with at least 70% cocoa solids, broken into pieces

4 large eggs

50g (1¾oz) caster sugar

zest of 1 orange, finely chopped

1 tbsp Urfa chilli flakes

75ml (2½fl oz) double cream

2 tbsp whipped cream, to serve (optional)

cocoa powder, to serve

Chocolate pots are something of a win-win dessert: easy to make and always a treat, so everybody's happy. These are enhanced with a hint of orange and Turkish Urfa chilli, or *Urfa biber*. Traditionally used as a seasoning for grilled meats, this fascinating chilli is sun-dried by day, then wrapped and sweated by night. The process creates a profound raisiny, earthy, chewy flavour, which lends itself beautifully to chocolate. It's not too spicy, but its heat grows in the mouth for an extraordinary piquant depth. It's widely available online or in good Middle Eastern and Turkish stores. You could substitute it with a good pinch of chilli powder, but you will lose its unique flavours.

Bring a saucepan of water to the boil. Place the chocolate into a large heatproof bowl, and sit it on top of the saucepan, making sure the bottom of the bowl does not touch the boiling water. Melt the chocolate gently, stirring every now and then.

Meanwhile, separate the eggs. Place the yolks in a clean bowl and beat with an electric whisk until creamy. Then beat in half the sugar.

When the chocolate has melted, remove from the heat and stir in the orange zest and Urfa pepper. Then stir in the cream thoroughly until the mixture is smooth and glossy. Add the egg yolks to the chocolate and fold together.

In a separate clean bowl, beat the egg whites to stiff peaks with an electric whisk. Then beat in the remaining sugar. Now fold the egg whites gently into the chocolate mixture with a spatula or metal spoon, taking care not to knock too much of the air out of them – the lighter your touch, the lighter the mousse.

Pour or spoon the mousse into six ramekins or demi-tasse cups and smooth them over. Cover with cling film or foil and pop them in the fridge for at least an hour to set. If you like, decorate each pot with a teaspoonful of whipped cream and a sprinkling of cocoa powder.

BAJA BLONDIES

MAKES 16–24

125g (4½oz) plain flour
large pinch of sea salt
2 tsp baking powder
2 tsp dried chipotle powder
90g (3oz) unsalted butter
250g (9oz) light brown sugar
1 tsp vanilla extract
2 large eggs, lightly beaten
100g (3½oz) pecans or walnuts,
chopped
125g (4½oz) stoned dates, chopped

Baja California is one of the 31 states of Mexico, but has a huge amount in common with its US neighbour to the north – thus the inspiration for the Baja Blondie! Sticky, sweet and spicy, it's a marriage of smoky Mexican chipotle chillies and all-American dates and pecans.

Once you've made these a couple of times, why not try a different chilli powder for a different 'chilli kick'? Ancho chilli would give a very mild, slightly fruity punch, while pasilla powder would give a little more heat but a lot more smoky earthiness. Enjoy!

Pre-heat the oven to 180°C, 350°F, gas mark 4 and line a 20cm (8in) square baking tin with non-stick baking paper.

In a large bowl, mix the flour, salt, baking powder and chipotle chilli powder. Set aside.

In a large saucepan over a low heat, melt the butter. When it is completely melted, remove from the heat and add the sugar and vanilla extract. When combined, add the eggs and stir in thoroughly. Now stir in the flour mixture, pecans or walnuts and the dates. Make sure you mix it all thoroughly.

Pour and scrape the mixture into the lined tin and bake in the oven for 25–30 minutes or until you can see cracks appearing. Don't overcook, as you want them gooey and sticky and they will carry on cooking as they cool.

Leave to cool in the tin. When completely cold, cut into 16 or 24 pieces – up to you!

PAVLOVA IN PURGATORY

SERVES 6–8

for the meringue

butter or oil, for greasing

plain flour, for dusting

3 large egg whites, at room temperature

175g (6oz) caster sugar

½ tsp vanilla extract

1 tsp cornflour, sifted, plus extra for dusting

¾ tsp white wine vinegar (to keep the meringue moist)

for the fruit topping

150g (5½oz) raspberries

1 tsp ground Kashmiri *mirch* or good-quality chilli powder of your choice

50g (1¾oz) icing sugar

25ml (1fl oz) fresh lemon juice

350–400g (12½–14oz) strawberries, hulled and cut into halves and quarters

for the cream filling

300ml (10½fl oz) double cream

½ tbsp caster sugar

1 drop of vanilla extract

If a pepper sauce makes something *diavolo*, why shouldn't a chilli-spiced sauce make something purgatorial? Especially since, in this case, the rich cream and meringue provide a path out of the fire. Pavlova's roots are Australian, while the raspberry-dressed strawberries come from the Italian dessert *fragole cardinale*, so this recipe is a nod to the many Italians who have made their home down under.

Pre-heat the oven to 120°C, 250°F, gas mark ½. Cut out a 20cm (8in) circle of non-stick baking paper. Grease it lightly and dust with cornflour, shaking off the excess. Place it on a baking sheet.

To make the meringue, use an electric whisk to beat the egg whites in a deep bowl until they just hold a peak. Gradually whisk in the sugar, a third at a time, and keep whisking until the mixture is very stiff and shiny. Fold in the vanilla extract, cornflour and vinegar.

Spoon the mix on to the prepared paper and spread it out to cover the paper entirely, making sure the edges are a little higher than the middle, to hold the filling. Bake for about 1½ hours, until the top and sides are slightly golden but the middle remains sticky. Remove from the oven and set aside to cool. Then gently remove the non-stick baking paper. Leave until cold.

To make the fruit topping, blitz the raspberries and chilli powder in a blender. Pass the mixture through a sieve into a medium bowl to remove the seeds. Stir in the icing sugar and lemon juice, then pour over the strawberries. Leave to marinate for at least an hour in the fridge before assembling the pavlova.

Now whip the cream to stiff peaks and stir in the caster sugar and vanilla extract. Spread liberally on top of the pavlova base. Top with the strawberries and some of their raspberry chilli sauce. Serve the remaining sauce in a jug on the side.

'COOL CHILE' BROWNIES
with ANCHO CARAMEL SAUCE

MAKES 12

for the 'Cool Chile' brownies

200g (7oz) dark chocolate, with at least 70% cocoa solids

250g (9oz) unsalted butter, cubed and at room temperature

65g (2¼oz) plain flour

1 tsp baking powder

80g (3oz) Mexican chocolate, grated

2 tsp diced pasilla chillies

300g (10½oz) caster sugar

4 large eggs, beaten

for the ancho caramel sauce (makes 200ml (7fl oz); optional)

100g (3½oz) palm sugar

100g (3½oz) unsalted butter

200ml (7fl oz) double cream

3 tsp dried ancho chilli powder

good pinch of salt

These spicy, sticky brownies, courtesy of the brilliant Kelly at the Cool Chile Company in London, are great on their own, but especially indulgent if drizzled with this chilli-spiked caramel sauce and served with soothing vanilla ice cream to make a Cool Chile sundae. If you'd prefer a smokier-tasting sauce, substitute the ancho chilli powder with 1–2 teaspoons of chipotle powder.

Mexican chocolate is flavoured with cinnamon and sometimes nutmeg, allspice and orange. The Cool Chile Company sells their own ready-grated version which is highly recommended and can be bought online. Please note that some brands contain nuts, so check carefully.

Pre-heat the oven to 180°C, 350°F, gas mark 4. Prepare a 25cm (10in) square baking tin or a 23 × 28cm (9 × 11in) roasting tray by lining the base and the sides with non-stick baking paper.

Break the dark chocolate into a heatproof bowl and add the cubed butter. Put the bowl over a saucepan of simmering water. Make sure the bowl can sit on the pan without touching the water. Melt the butter and chocolate together – you want them smooth and glossy – and remove from the heat once melted. Set aside.

In a separate bowl, sift together the flour and baking powder. Then add the grated Mexican chocolate, diced pasilla chillies and sugar, and stir all the dry ingredients together. When they're well combined, add them to the melted butter and chocolate mixture. Finally, add the beaten eggs. Mix it all together until you have a shiny and silky batter.

Pour the batter into the baking tin and bake in the oven for about 25 minutes, or until crispy on top but still gooey in the middle. Leave to cool in the tin, then cut into squares and remove.

If you want to make the caramel sauce, put the sugar and butter in a pan and melt them together over a low heat. As soon as they've melted and amalgamated, add the cream, ancho powder and salt. Now stir and bring back to a simmer. Keep stirring and bubbling until it turns lovely and golden, which will take 4–6 minutes.

Serve the brownies on their own or with scoops of vanilla ice cream and a generous drizzling of the hot caramel sauce, if you wish.

COCONUT CHILLI TREACLE TART

SERVES 8

for the pastry

110g (4oz) unsalted butter, cold and cubed, plus extra for greasing

225g (8oz) plain flour

large pinch of sea salt

small glass of ice water

for the filling

450g (1lb) golden syrup

2 tbsp fresh lemon or lime juice

50g (1¾oz) breadcrumbs

1–2 tsp roasted dried chilli flakes (to taste)

50g (1¾oz) unsweetened desiccated coconut

This sweet, sticky treacle tart is perked up with lemon juice and a kick of dried chilli. There's also some coconut in there to make it chewy, just like my memory of childhood toffee! It's delicious served with a coconut ice cream or sorbet.

Pre-heat the oven to 190°C, 375°F, gas mark 5 and grease a 23cm (9in) round tart tin with a removable base.

In a large bowl, rub the butter and flour together with your fingertips until it has the texture of fine breadcrumbs. Mix in the salt, then add the ice water, a teaspoonful at a time, until the pastry comes together into a nice smooth ball. Try not to handle it too much as it may go tough.

Gently press the pastry into the tin with your fingertips until it evenly covers the bottom and sides. Line the pastry case with non-stick baking paper, fill with baking beans and blind bake for 10–12 minutes. Being careful not to burn yourself, remove the paper and beans from the tart case and place it back in the oven for 5–8 minutes.

Meanwhile, melt together the syrup and juice in a small saucepan and heat gently, stirring until well combined. Mix together the breadcrumbs, chilli and coconut, and add to the syrup mixture. Stir well and remove from the heat.

Fill the tart case with the syrup mixture and bake in the oven for 20–25 minutes, until golden brown. Serve warm with coconut ice cream or sorbet.

CHILLI BASIL MOJITO

SERVES 1

7 Thai sweet basil leaves

7 fresh mint leaves, and an extra one to garnish

1 fat slice of Thai long red chilli or any mild red chilli

crushed ice, to fill the glass

4 tsp sugar syrup

2 tbsp fresh lime juice

50ml (1¾ fl oz) white rum

soda water, to top up

Cuba meets Thailand in an icy glass with an added chilli kick. If you can't find Thai basil, you can substitute regular basil, but the drink will lack that extra aniseed flavour.

Place the basil, mint and chilli in the bottom of a glass and crush them together with a muddler or the wrong end of a wooden spoon. Fill the glass with ice, then add the sugar syrup, lime juice and rum. Stir it all together, then top up with soda water.

THAI MICHELADA

SERVES 1

2 limes

sea salt, to rim the glass

sliver of Thai bird's-eye chilli, plus 2 whole Thai bird's-eye chillies, to garnish

ice cubes, to fill the glass

nam pla (fish sauce), to taste

Sriracha hot sauce, to taste

soy sauce, to taste

50ml (1¾ fl oz) tomato juice

freshly ground white pepper

Thai beer, to top up

Michelada is a Mexican *cerveza preparada* – prepared beer. (Think of it as a beery Bloody Mary!) This Thai-inspired version is very much a collision of two chilli-heavy food cultures. Sriracha, Thailand's famous hot ketchup, is readily available to buy in the UK and adds an extra punch to the white pepper, while the *nam pla* (fish sauce) adds an enhancing saltiness.

Juice 1½ limes and cut the final lime half into 4 pieces. Wipe one of the pieces around the rim of a tall, frosty glass and run the rim through the sea salt so it sticks to the edge. Now put the chilli sliver and lime pieces in the glass and crush together with a muddler or the back of a spoon. Fill the glass with ice. Pour in the lime juice, then add the sauces and tomato juice. Season with white pepper and stir everything together, then top up with cold Thai beer. Spear the bird's-eye chillies with a cocktail stick, balance them atop the glass and serve.

CONTINUED ▶

▶ CONTINUED FROM PREVIOUS PAGE

TANGMO TANGO

SERVES 1

400g (14oz) watermelon, plus a thin wedge to garnish

slice of Thai long red chilli or serrano chilli

ice cubes, to fill the glass

25ml (1fl oz) Mekhong Thai whisky or the amber rum of your choice

dash of angostura bitters

squeeze of fresh lime juice

mint leaf, to garnish

Tangmo is the Thai word for watermelon, which gives this refreshing drink its sweetness. It's given an added boost by the chilli, mint and lime, and some alcoholic zing by the Mekhong Thai whisky, a unique product which is actually more akin to a rum ... even though they call it whisky. It is distilled from a mixture of sugar cane and rice, giving it a distinct flavour. If you can't find it, replace with an amber rum.

First, prepare the watermelon. Remove the rind and as many seeds as you can. You should end up with about 225g (8oz) of flesh. Then put the watermelon flesh in a blender and blitz until smooth. Pass the watermelon juice through a sieve, using a spoon to push it through, to remove any excess pulp. You should now have 150ml (5fl oz) of juice.

In the bottom of a Collins glass, crush the chilli with a muddler or the back of a spoon. Fill the glass with ice, then pour in the Mekhong whisky or the rum. Add the watermelon juice, a splash of angostura bitters and a squeeze of lime. Stir everything together. Then twist a mint leaf over the glass to release its oils and float it on the top. Garnish with the watermelon wedge and serve.

DIRTY CHILLI BLOODY MARY

SERVES 1

ice cubes, to fill the glass
4 tbsp vodka
tomato juice, to top up
Tabasco sauce, to taste
Worcestershire sauce, to taste
2 lemon wedges
good splash of chilli pickling juice
1 celery stick, to garnish
1–2 pickled chillies, to garnish
celery salt and freshly ground
black pepper

You can't talk about chilli-based drinks without mentioning the Bloody Mary. It's packed with all that spicy goodness to chase away the very worst hangover. Everyone who makes them has their own secret recipe; some make it as hot as possible, others make it as alcoholic as possible. This one takes the notion behind a dirty martini – that you add some olive water along with the green olive garnish – and applies it here. The pickled chillies take the olive's place as a garnish, and their pickling juice provides the spicy 'dirt'. Fiery stuff!

Fill a tall glass with ice and pour in the vodka. Season with celery salt and black pepper, then top up with tomato juice. Now get spicy with the Tabasco and Worcestershire sauce, adding them a splash at a time to taste. Squeeze in the juice of 1 lemon wedge, add the chilli pickling juice and stir everything together with the celery stick. Then spear the pickled chillies and the second lemon wedge with a cocktail stick and lay them across the top of the glass. Serve immediately.

RELISHES AND PICKLES

NAM PLA PRIK

MAKES 4 tablespoons (enough for one sitting)

4 tbsp *nam pla* (fish sauce)

8–10 Thai bird's-eye chillies, thinly sliced

1 garlic clove, peeled and thinly sliced (optional)

¼ lime, thinly sliced, then cut into segments (optional)

This is the quintessential Thai condiment, adding salt and heat to whatever you choose, including many of the Thai recipes in this book, such as the Spicy Seafood Soup (page 29), Drunkard's Beef Fried Rice (page 94) and Stir-fried Asparagus with Yellow Beans and Chilli (page 100). It's very simple and easy to make but it doesn't keep, so it's best to whip up as needed.

Measure the *nam pla* into a small serving bowl and add the remaining ingredients. Leave to stand for an hour or so before use.

SIMPLE HARISSA

MAKES 100ml (3½fl oz)

3–4 garlic cloves, peeled

½ tsp sea salt

3 tbsp cumin seeds, toasted

1 tbsp coriander seeds, toasted

6 dried African bird's-eye piri-piri chillies

3 tbsp cayenne pepper

6–8 tbsp olive oil

handful of fresh coriander, roughly chopped (optional)

Harissa can be found across North Africa and in the markets of southern France. The cayenne, from French Guiana, packs a punch, but don't skimp on it. Stir harissa into soups, traditional tagines and stews, or serve on the side of grills or roasted meat.

Pound together the garlic, salt, cumin seeds, coriander seeds and dried chillies in a pestle and mortar until they form a smooth paste. Add the cayenne pepper and olive oil, and stir until combined. Add the chopped coriander, if you're using it. Taste and add more salt, if you like. This harissa will keep for up to a week.

SPICY BARBECUE SAUCE

MAKES approx. 500ml (18fl oz)

6 heaped tbsp plum jam, ideally without peel

6 heaped tbsp caster sugar

6 tbsp tomato ketchup

6 tbsp Worcestershire sauce

4 tbsp oyster sauce

4 tsp Tabasco sauce

1 chipotle in adobo sauce and 2 tbsp of the sauce

1 tbsp malt or cider vinegar

2 tsp dried mustard powder

1 tsp liquid hickory smoke

salt and freshly ground black pepper

This sauce was inspired by a recipe from an old family friend, Alan Burrough. Of course, I've chillied it up since I got my hands on it. The earthy fire of the chipotle is enhanced by the touch of liquid smoke (see page 120), making this the perfect foil for pulled pork and an excellent condiment for a summer barbecue. This recipe makes plenty, so have some sterilised jars at the ready to store it.

Mix all of the ingredients together in a blender at low speed until they amalgamate. Then pour everything into a small saucepan. Add 3 tablespoons of water and place over a low to medium heat until it comes to the boil. Reduce the heat and allow to simmer for 5–8 minutes. Then decant into sterilised jars and leave to cool before using or storing in the fridge. It will keep for up to 3 weeks – if you can resist it for that long.

TIP

To sterilise jars, first wash them and their lids in hot soapy water. Rinse thoroughly in fresh hot water and set aside to dry. Then either bring a large stock pot of water to the boil over a medium hob, put the jars and lids in, and boil them for a good 10 minutes, or put the jars in a clean roasting tin and bake in a pre-heated 160°C, 325°F, gas mark 3 oven for 10–15 minutes (though not the lids because they often have plastic inside them – lids should always be boiled). Remove from the boiling water or oven with clean tongs and set aside on clean tea towels to dry, or use straight away. Do not touch with your fingers.

A TRIO OF NAM PRIKS

Nam prik means 'chilli water', but really these are relishes or dips – they swing between the two, making it hard to translate the term precisely. They're often served with very lightly blanched Chinese cabbage and green beans, squares of omelette, and *kap moo* – Thai deep-fried pork skin. You can buy *kap moo* at most Thai supermarkets, or use prawn crackers as an alternative. *Nam priks* are terrific as a starter platter before an Asian meal, or to have with drinks and canapés.

NAM PRIK ONG

MAKES approx. 175g (6oz)

2 tbsp vegetable oil

2 Thai shallots or 1 regular shallot, peeled and finely chopped

3 garlic cloves, peeled and finely chopped

½ heaped tbsp good-quality red curry paste

125g (4½oz) minced pork

2 tomatoes, chopped

1 tbsp tomato purée (optional)

1–2 tbsp *nam pla* (fish sauce)

1–2 tbsp fresh lime juice (from approx. 1 lime)

1 tsp caster sugar

NORTHERN STYLE PORK DIP

This is a fairly mild *nam prik*, both sweet with tomatoes and also intensely savoury. The chilli element is introduced via the red curry paste. Make sure you buy the best quality paste you can.

Heat the oil in a wok over a high heat, until it shimmers. Add the shallots, followed by the garlic, and fry, stirring all the time, until golden brown. Mix in the curry paste and cook until fragrant, about a minute or so. Add the pork and stir-fry until it's cooked through. Add the tomato and stir through. If your tomatoes are a little anaemic, add the tomato purée for an extra intensity of flavour. Then quickly add the *nam pla*, lime juice and sugar. Stir-fry for a couple of minutes. Taste and adjust the seasoning. Then serve warm in a small bowl.

TIP

If your tomatoes are not ripe and sweet enough, deploy the tomato purée.

CONTINUED ▶

▶ CONTINUED FROM PREVIOUS PAGE

NAM PRIK NUM

MAKES approx. 250g (9oz)

2–4 Thai round aubergines, topped, tailed and halved

6 Thai green *prik num* chillies or any mild–medium long green chillies, halved

8 garlic cloves, peeled

4 Thai shallots, peeled and halved or 2 normal shallots, peeled and quartered

2 coriander roots (see Tip, page 89)

pinch of sugar

2–3 tbsp *nam pla* (fish sauce)

juice of ½ lime

pinch of sea salt

GRILLED CHILLI AND AUBERGINE NAM PRIK

When I lived in Bangkok, one of our neighbours ran a family business making this *nam prik num*, roasting all the ingredients over charcoal fires. The smell was pungent, to say the least, the nose-burning scent of chillies filling the air. So, to make up for any discomfort they may have caused us, they'd hang plastic bags of it on our front gate as a gift. It was delicious – smoky, spicy, sour and sweet – a real taste of Thailand. Even now, when I'm making this, the smell takes me straight back, though without the rivers of tears!

Traditionally this is made with *prik num*, which are long, light-green, chillies from Northern Thailand. As you can imagine, they are not easy to find, so for many years I have used what I could — basically, any long green chilli. Not everyone includes aubergine in their version, but I prefer to.

In separate foil parcels, cook each vegetable and the coriander roots over a medium heat in a dry frying pan until soft – for about 15 minutes – turning them from time to time. You want them to take on a grilled-like colouring, so open the parcels occasionally to see how they're doing. This is the best way to replicate the direct heat you'd get from an open fire.

Once they're cooked, let them cool slightly. Then pound them together, with a good pinch of salt, in a pestle and mortar or pulse them in a blender or small food processor. You want to end up with a chunky, textured dip.

Place into a small bowl. Add a pinch of sugar, the *nam pla* and the lime juice, and stir them in well. Taste for balance and serve. It will keep for a couple of days, at most.

NAM PRIK KAPI

MAKES 200–250ml (7–9fl oz)

2 tbsp shrimp paste

12 Thai garlic cloves *or* 6 regular garlic cloves, peeled

9 Thai bird's-eye chillies, plus extra to garnish

25g (1oz) pea aubergines (about 20)

5 tbsp fresh lime juice (from approx. 2–3 limes)

1 tbsp *nam pla* (fish sauce)

1½ tbsp dried shrimp, whizzed in a blender

1 tbsp palm sugar

1–2 tbsp warm water, to adjust consistency (optional)

SHRIMP PASTE DIP

Shrimp paste forms the backbone of a lot of Thai dishes, particularly in the south. It has an intensely deep, earthy flavour. So this *nam prik* tastes quintessentially Thai. In fact, all the ingredients in this recipe make up the core of Thai flavours. It is spicy and pungent.

The pea aubergine (or turkey berry) is a small aubergine which you can find fairly easily in most Asian stores. If you can't find it, just leave out.

First, roast the shrimp paste: wrap it in some foil and heat it in a dry wok or frying pan over a low to medium hob for 3–5 minutes, turning once. This really releases its flavour.

In a large, heavy pestle and mortar, pound the garlic, shrimp paste and chillies together until you get a smooth paste. Add half the pea aubergines and crush gently. Then add the lime juice, *nam pla*, dried shrimp and palm sugar, and mix thoroughly. Add the rest of the pea aubergines and stir through. Add a little warm water, if needed – you want a soft dropping consistency.

Place in a small bowl and garnish with extra bird's-eye chillies.

MARIA'S FRESH TOMATILLO SALSA

MAKES approx. 225ml (8fl oz)

200g (7oz) fresh tomatillos, papery skins removed, flesh washed and chopped

1 garlic clove, peeled

2 jalapeño chillies, seeded and chopped

good handful of fresh coriander

pinch of sugar

sea salt, to taste

In downtown LA, I tasted this incredibly vibrant, almost Kermit-green salsa made by a street vendor from Puebla in Mexico. Her secret was to use raw tomatillos. Once you make it, serve it as soon as you can to preserve its incredible colour. This is delicious drizzled over enchiladas and tacos. Or try it with the Cuban Black Bean Soup on page 46.

Blitz everything in a blender, then season with salt and sugar. Add a dash of water if necessary, to loosen the salsa. Serve as soon as possible; it will keep for no more than a day.

HARI CHUTNEY

GREEN CHILLI AND CORIANDER 'CHUTNEY'

MAKES approx. 100ml (3½fl oz)

80g bunch coriander, chopped roughly

4 *hari mirch* green finger chillies, chopped

3–4 slices of green mango or sharp green eating apple, peeled (approx. 40g (1½oz) after peeling)

3–4 tbsp fresh lemon or lime juice

1–2 garlic cloves, peeled and crushed

1 tsp cumin seeds, toasted

1 tsp sugar

1 tsp sea salt

This isn't a chutney in the English sense, since it's not cooked. It is a classic Indian table salsa: quick to make, tart and highly spiced with *hari mirch* chillies. Serve with curries, grills, pekoras, samosas or the Kashmiri-style Grilled Chicken on page 111.

Put everything in a blender and blitz until smooth. Add some water, a tablespoon at a time, if it sticks – just to make it easier to blend. Taste and adjust the salt, lemon and chilli ratio to suit your palate.

Make this as close as possible to the time you want to serve it. It will keep for up to 2 days in the fridge, though its fresh green colour may fade.

ROMESCO SAUCE

MAKES approx. 400ml (14fl oz)

2 large tomatoes

1 Romano pepper, halved and seeded

100ml (3½fl oz) olive oil, plus 4 tbsp

1 head of garlic, left unpeeled

100g (3½oz) blanched almonds

1 slice of white bread, torn into small pieces (sourdough is good)

4 piquillo peppers, from a jar

2 dried ñora peppers, soaked for 2–3 hours, then drained, seeded and roughly chopped

1 heaped tsp hot smoked paprika

1–2 tbsp sherry vinegar, to taste

sea salt and freshly ground pepper

From Catalonia in north-eastern Spain, this stars the sun-dried ñora pepper, a fat, glossy chilli with a deep red colour. It's essential to the recipe, imbuing it with a soft, mild warmth and a distinctive sweet flavour that's all its own. You can find it at Spanish or Mediterranean delis, or buy it online. It needs to be soaked for a few hours before use. Serve this Romesco sauce with grilled asparagus, pan-fried scallops, chargrilled lamb or sea bass.

Pre-heat the oven to 180°C, 350°F, gas mark 4.

Cut the tomatoes in half, season with salt and pepper, and place in a roasting tin with the Romano pepper. Drizzle with 2 tablespoons of the olive oil.

Wrap the garlic head in foil and add it to the tin. Pop the tin in the oven and roast for 25–30 minutes, until the tomatoes are soft and the pepper has taken on some colour and is soft as well. You may want to turn the pepper halves, once or twice. Remove from the oven and set aside to cool. Leave the oven turned on.

Place the almonds on another baking tray and pop in the oven for 5–8 minutes, until just toasted – be careful they do not burn. Set aside to cool.

Heat 2 tablespoons of olive oil in a frying pan over a medium hob and fry the bread gently until browned and crispy. Set aside on kitchen paper to drain.

Pop the garlic cloves out of their skins and place in a blender or food processor with everything else except the 100ml (3½fl oz) olive oil and the vinegar. Now blitz, being careful to retain some texture, and adding the rest of the olive oil gradually as you go. Add sherry vinegar to taste, and season with salt and pepper to taste as well. Serve immediately.

ROUILLE

MAKES approx. 250ml (9fl oz)

splash of hot water
6–8 fat garlic cloves, peeled
good pinch of sea salt
2 large fresh egg yolks
250ml (9fl oz) extra-virgin olive oil
½ tsp saffron threads
pinch of cayenne pepper
pinch of ground chilli peppers

Translated literally as 'rust', this ochre-coloured variant of aïoli is simply fantastic. Using a pestle and mortar will give a better texture, and the ritual is wonderfully calming. But you can use a hand-whisk, blender or whatever you prefer.

Serve with croutons alongside bouillabaisse or fish soups, or as a dip for raw vegetables, with some good bread and a crisp white wine.

Before you begin, make sure your eggs are at room temperature. The colder they are, the more likely your rouille will split. Warm a mortar with a splash of hot water and dry well. Crush the garlic in the mortar with the sea salt, getting it as smooth as you can. Add the egg yolks and combine, stirring and pressing – it is said that you should always stir in the same direction to avoid the mixture splitting.

When you have a silky amalgamated mixture, start adding the olive oil, a drop at a time, stirring and pressing constantly, until you have a mixture that is thin but still holding together. Then add the saffron, cayenne and ground chilli pepper and carry on adding the oil. Once the mixture has thickened and starts to feel more 'jellyish', you can add more of the oil, in a thin stream, continuing to stir and beat until it has a wobbly, creamy mayonnaise texture. You may not need to use all the oil.

Taste and adjust the seasoning. Serve at room temperature. This can be refrigerated for a couple of days – if it doesn't all get eaten at once!

MO'BAY MANGO CHUTNEY

WEAR GLOVES
FOR THIS ONE

MAKES approx. 3 litres
(5½ pints)

12 firm mangoes, peeled and chopped – they should be just approaching ripe (approx. 4kg (9lb) unpeeled; 2.25kg (5lb) peeled)

1kg (2¼lb) brown sugar

750ml (1¼ pints) malt vinegar

12 Scotch bonnet chillies, seeded and cut into strips

1 large onion, peeled and chopped

1 large or 3 small ripe tomatoes, chopped

½ red sweet pepper, seeded and chopped

½ green sweet pepper, seeded and chopped

6×1.5cm (3×¾in) fresh root ginger, peeled and chopped

2 garlic cloves, peeled and chopped

1 tsp salt

200g (7oz) raisins

This mango chutney comes from Aunty Toops, one of the great matriarchs of my husband's family in Montego Bay. It's a recipe that has been handed down orally and it's quite loosey-goosey: if you don't have light brown sugar, use dark; if you don't have malt vinegar, use just distilled white vinegar. It's very much based around what might be available in the store cupboard. Note the liberal use of fiery, fruity Scotch bonnet. This chutney goes with curries, cold meats, pork pies, jerk chicken, cheese . . . anything!

Place all the ingredients apart from the raisins in a large, sturdy pan. Bring to the boil over a medium heat and then turn down to a simmer, stirring often, and cook, uncovered, for about 30 minutes, or until the mango has softened slightly.

Remove from the heat and let cool a little. Carefully ladle half of the mixture into a blender or food processor and pulse a couple of times until blended but retaining some texture. It will be VERY HOT so be cautious.

Return to the pan and bring back to the boil. Turn the heat down to low, and simmer gently for 4–5 minutes. Remove from the heat, add the raisins and stir through. Then pour into hot sterilised jars (see Tip, page 193).

Allow to cool completely and store in a cool, dark place, or in the fridge, for at least a week before opening. This will keep for up to a year in a cool cupboard or in the fridge once opened.

ZHUG

MAKES about 130ml (4½fl oz)

3 *hari mirch* green finger chillies, halved and seeded

3–4 green African bird's-eye chillies

10 green cardamom pods, seeds only

1 tsp caraway seeds

1 tsp cumin seeds

1 tbsp cracked black peppercorns

4 garlic cloves, peeled

large bunch of coriander

2 tbsp chopped flat-leaf parsley

80ml (2–3fl oz) extra-virgin olive oil

good squeeze of fresh lime juice, to taste

sea salt

Originating in Yemen and hugely popular in Israel, this bright-green, citrus-fresh and spicy condiment is seen more and more internationally. Serve as a dip with fresh flatbreads and strained yoghurt, or on the side of grills and roasts. You can replace the African bird's-eyes with Thai bird's-eyes, if necessary.

Put the chillies in a food processor or blender with the spices, garlic, coriander and parsley. Slowly add the olive oil with the motor running until you have a fairly loose sauce a bit like pesto. Taste, and add a generous squeeze of lime juice and salt to your liking. Serve immediately.

A GLOBAL MEDLEY OF SALSA VERDE

Salsa verde literally means 'green sauce'. Often it's spiked with chillies, and it has a multitude of uses. Here are a few regional versions from around the world. For a typically Mexican *salsa verde*, see the recipe for Green Chilli with Pork on page 51.

ARGENTINE CHIMICHURRI

MAKES 175–200ml (6–7fl oz)

80g (3oz) flat-leaf parsley, stalks trimmed off

2 tbsp fresh oregano leaves

4 garlic cloves, peeled and finely chopped

1 bird's-eye chilli, seeded and finely chopped, or 1–2 tsp dried chilli flakes, or a combination of both

10 tbsp olive oil

2 tbsp red wine vinegar

salt and freshly ground pepper

No one knows exactly why this green sauce is called chimichurri. One theory claims it's a corruption of the name Jimmy McCurry, who was either an Irish meat wholesaler or a fighter in the Argentine War of Independence. Whether or not he invented it, the story doesn't say, but it's fun to imagine he devised the sauce to go with a fabulous piece of Argentine beef grilled over his pampas campfire. Either way, it's delicious.

There are loads of different versions, some with cumin, some with fresh coriander and others with finely chopped onion. It is often made with dried chillies, but this recipe uses a hot fresh chilli. As with all *salsas verdes*, you're unlikely to find two regional variants that are the same.

Finely chop the parsley and oregano and place in a bowl. Add the chopped garlic and chilli – fresh or dried – then add the olive oil, vinegar and salt and pepper to taste. Mix together and let it sit at room temperature for at least 30 minutes before using.

You can keep this for up to a day, but it's best used immediately.

THAI SALSA VERDE

MAKES 80–100ml (3–3½fl oz)

leaves from 1 large bunch of coriander, chopped finely

3 garlic cloves, peeled and chopped

4 green Thai bird's-eye chillies, chopped

2 coriander roots (see Tip, page 89)

3½–4 tbsp fresh lime juice (from 2–3 limes)

2 tbsp *nam pla* (fish sauce)

1 tsp sugar

Heavy with coriander and Thailand's signature bird's-eye chillies, this vibrantly green and spicy sauce is fantastic with grilled or steamed fish, grilled chicken or raw sushi-grade salmon. This is at its best made and served at once.

Place all the sauce ingredients into a blender (or a small herb chopper as the blades are just the right size) and whoosh until fairly smooth. Pop into a dish and serve at once.

ITALIAN SALSA VERDE WITH CHILLI

MAKES 80–100ml (3–3½fl oz)

5 garlic cloves, peeled

50g (1¾oz) tinned anchovies

½ ciliegia piccante or medium hot red chilli, seeded and finely chopped

1 tbsp salted capers, rinsed

20g (¾oz) flat-leaf parsley leaves

20g (¾oz) fresh mint leaves

20g (¾oz) fresh basil leaves

50–75ml (1¾–2½fl oz) extra-virgin olive oil

fresh lemon juice, to taste

sea salt and freshly ground black pepper

Gorgeous, green and heavy with herbs, this is easy to make and goes with everything from fish to steak. This version is mildly spiced. Some folks add chopped boiled eggs or crushed potatoes, so feel free to play around.

Chop the garlic, anchovies, chilli, capers and herbs, either by hand or by pulsing them in a food processor – just make sure you don't make it *too* sloppy: this *salsa verde* should have a little heft to it.

Add olive oil and lemon juice to taste (you may not need all the olive oil, it's up to you), and stir through. Season with salt and pepper, and serve immediately.

WEAR GLOVES
FOR THIS ONE

**MAKES approx. 1.5 litres
(2½ pints)**

450–500g (1lb–1lb 2oz) mixed chillies
600ml (1 pint) distilled white vinegar
4 garlic cloves, peeled
2 tbsp coriander seeds
2 tbsp black peppercorns
2 bay leaves
1 tbsp caster sugar
1 tbsp salt

QUICK PICKLED CHILLIES

When I say 'quick', I *mean* quick – you can use these after about 24 hours of pickling. Of course, they get better and better with time, but sometimes you need them . . . fast. They go really well with cheese or cold meats. Or they can be chopped through salads and dressings. You will need sterilised jars at the ready for this recipe (see Tip, page 193). Make sure they are good, heatproof ones.

Wash the chillies thoroughly in some well-salted water, drain and set aside to dry.

One by one, pierce the chillies with a fork and place them into sterilised jars. If you have any larger chillies, slice them into fat chunks and add to the jars too. Set aside.

Combine all the other ingredients in a saucepan with 600ml (1 pint) of water and bring to the boil over a medium heat, then let it simmer for 6–8 minutes.

Carefully pour the hot liquid into the jars over the chillies and seal the jars tightly. Cool and refrigerate. Store the pickled chillies in the fridge once opened.

A MEDLEY OF RED SALSAS

Red salsas or sauces, like their herb-laden green counterparts, provide excellent spicy accents to all kinds of dishes, from enchiladas to soups, tacos or even your eggs at breakfast. They can be cooked or uncooked, fiery or mild.

SALSA ROJA

MAKES approx. 800ml (1½ pints)

4–5 guajillo chillies, seeded, de-veined and de-stemmed

4–5 ancho chillies, seeded, de-veined and de-stemmed

1 *chile de árbol*, seeded and de-stemmed (optional)

4 garlic cloves, peeled and chopped

1 small onion, peeled and chopped

2 large tomatoes, peeled and chopped

800ml (1½ pints) light chicken or vegetable stock or water

½ tbsp dried Mexican oregano (or normal oregano will do)

1 tsp ground cumin

sea salt, to taste

There are many versions of this simple red sauce, primarily used for enchiladas. Here, the earthy heat of the guajillo chilli balances out the sweeter fruitiness of the ancho, combining for a wonderfully savoury and spicy sauce.

Over a medium heat, toast the chillies in a dry frying pan for a few minutes on either side, until just fragrant – don't let them burn. Remove from the heat and transfer to a large saucepan. Add all the remaining ingredients, stir together, and bring to the boil over a medium heat. Turn the heat down very low, partially cover and simmer the sauce for 25–30 minutes, until the chillies are soft and yielding, stirring every now and then. Remove from the heat and let cool a little before pouring into a food processor or blender and blitzing until smooth. Taste and add more salt, if needed.

Serve liberally over the Quick Baked Chicken Enchiladas on page 119 as an alternative to teh sauce given there, as a sauce with your eggs in the morning or on the side of grilled chicken or steak. It will keep in the fridge for a day or two.

MEXICAN ROASTED TOMATO SAUCE

MAKES approx. 600ml (1 pint)

600g (1lb 5oz) tomatoes, halved
1 jalapeño chilli, halved
1 serrano chilli, halved
1 small onion, peeled and roughly chopped
2 garlic cloves, peeled
2 tbsp vegetable oil
juice of ½ lime
handful of fresh coriander, chopped
sea salt

This is a really simple sauce, which is terrific with the Chilles Rellenos on page 208. It's also good with eggs and beans for a simple version of the classic Mexican breakfast, *huevos rancheros*, or 'ranchers' eggs'.

Note that you can regulate the heat of this sauce by choosing to leave the chilli seeds in or out. I prefer to leave them in here – the extra heat goes beautifully with the sweet tomatoes.

Pre-heat the oven to 180°C, 350°F, gas mark 4. Place the tomatoes, chillies, onion and garlic into a roasting tin, drizzle them with 1 tablespoon of the vegetable oil and sprinkle with a pinch of salt. Bake in the oven for 40 minutes or until the tomatoes are soft and collapsing. .

Now put everything from the roasting tin into a blender or food processor and blitz into a sauce. *Be careful not to overfill the blender – it will be hot and you don't want to burn yourself.* Add the lime juice and the coriander and quickly give it another pulse.

Heat the remaining oil in a saucepan over a medium heat. When it's hot, add the tomato sauce and cook until it has thickened slightly – about 5 minutes. Taste and add more salt, if needed. It should be sweet, a little spicy and tart.

This will keep for a few days in the fridge.

CONTINUED ▶

MEXICAN SALSA FRESCA

MAKES approx. 450g (1lb)

4 medium tomatoes, finely chopped

1 medium red onion, peeled and finely chopped

2–3 jalapeños, seeded and finely chopped

1 garlic clove, peeled and finely chopped (optional)

handful of coriander leaves, chopped

juice of ½ lime, or to taste

good pinch of sea salt

This is exactly what it says – a fresh salsa. It's the classic combination of tomatoes, red onion, coriander, lime and chillies that perks up so many things – enchiladas, meat and rice dishes. And it's the perfect dip for corn tortilla chips. If you like a bit more heat, you can leave the seeds in one of the jalapeños. This salsa is best made and served as fresh as possible, or you risk it becoming a little oniony.

Mix all the ingredients together in a medium-sized bowl. Let stand for 10–15 minutes. Taste and adjust seasoning. Serve immediately.

MEXICAN SALSA NEGRA

MAKES approx. 300ml (10½fl oz)

6 tbsp vegetable oil

50g (1¾oz) dried morita or chipotle chillies

hot water, to cover

6–8 garlic cloves, peeled

1 heaped tsp palm sugar

salt

This is a smoky, dark, almost chocolatey sauce, and deceptively simple to make. It gives so many dishes a real kick in the pants. The morita chilli is a variant of the chipotle. It's a dried red-ripe jalapeño which has been smoked for less time than a typical chipotle, leaving it softer and slightly fruitier.

Heat 3 tablespoons of the oil in a large frying pan over a medium hob. Add the moritas or chipotles, turning them occasionally until they puff up and are slightly more browned. This shouldn't take more than 4–5 minutes. Remove and place in a bowl. Cover with hot water and set aside for 25–30 minutes, or until the chillies are soft.

Meanwhile, reheat the oil over a low–medium hob and sauté the garlic cloves until golden, turning them often to be sure they don't burn. This should take 2 minutes. Remove from the oil and set aside.

Once the chillies have softened, drain them over another bowl, reserving the soaking water. Now remove the stems, seeds and any veins from the chillies and chop them up. Put them in a blender or food processor with 250ml (9fl oz) of the soaking water and the sautéed garlic and blitz into a smooth purée.

Heat the remaining 3 tablespoons of oil in a frying pan over a medium–high hob. When hot, add the sauce – you want it to sizzle – and stir well for a couple of minutes. Turn down the heat and let the sauce cook for 10–15 minutes, until thick and glossy.

Remove from the heat. Add the palm sugar and scrape back into the food processor, then blitz again. Add salt to taste. Set the sauce aside to cool.

Serve with grilled or roasted meats or pulled pork, or mixed into fresh tomato salsas, guacamole, ketchup, beans, soups and stews. It will keep in the fridge for up to 3 weeks.

CUCUMBER KIMCHEE

MAKES approx. 450g (1lb)

1 large cucumber or 2–3 small Persian cucumbers

1 tbsp sea salt

3 garlic cloves, peeled and finely chopped

4cm (1½in) fresh root ginger, peeled and finely chopped

3 large spring onions, sliced

2 tbsp *gochu garu* chilli powder

2–3 tbsp rice vinegar

2 tsp sugar

1–2 tsp *nam pla* (fish sauce) or a mix of soy and *nam pla*

1 tbsp toasted sesame seeds, plus extra to garnish

CHILLI FACT

This recipe uses *gochu garu* powder (*gochu* means 'chilli pepper' in Korean, and *garu* means 'powder'). It comes in different grinds, from coarse to fine, and its preparation is unique to Korea. It's fruitier and sweeter than cayenne or other ground peppers, and its vibrant red colour makes it really stand out. It is readily available in most Asian stores or online.

There are lots of different types of kimchee, or fermented vegetables. In the West, we're most familiar with the cabbage one, which ferments for days to achieve its proper flavour. This is a fresh, delicious and quick version, designed to deliver those pungent pickled flavours without the wait. It is brilliant with barbecue or rice dishes, or blitzed and stirred through a salad.

Halve the cucumber(s) down their length, then cut them across into fairly thick slices. Place them in a bowl and mix well with the salt. Now place the cucumber into a colander and leave to drain for about 40 minutes. Then rinse off the salt with cold water and dry the cucumber pieces well.

Put the cucumber in a clean, medium-sized, non-reactive bowl and add the garlic, ginger and spring onions, mixing well after each addition. Add the chilli powder, vinegar, sugar, *nam pla*, or the *nam pla* and soy mixture, and the sesame seeds. Mix well and cover. Set aside for at least 30 minutes and up to two hours before eating. Sprinkle with the extra sesame seeds before serving. It will keep, covered, in the fridge, for up to 3 days.

A TRIO OF CHILLI BUTTERS

Chilli Lime Butter

100g (3½oz) unsalted butter, softened

zest of 1 lime

½ tsp chilli flakes

pinch of sea salt

Smoky Chilli Butter

100g (3½oz) unsalted butter, softened

1 tsp dried chipotle powder or Urfa pepper

pinch of sea salt

pinch of sugar

Chilli Honey Butter

100g (3½oz) unsalted butter, softened

1 tbsp clear honey

1 serrano or jalapeño chilli, seeded and finely chopped, or 1 chipotle in adobo sauce, finely chopped

pinch of sea salt

Chilli-flavoured butter is a brilliant way to add a little extra heat to your food. Serve with steaks, corn on the cob, cornbread – you name it.

Place the butter and the flavourings in a bowl, and mush together until well combined. If you're making this to use with bread or the cornbread on page 153, you can simply serve it now. Otherwise spoon out on to cling film and roll into a cylinder of 3cm (1½in) in diameter and chill until firm. Peel away the cling film and cut off slices as needed. The butter will keep in the fridge for up to a week (depending on the freshness of your butter), and in the freezer for up to a month.

KNOW YOUR CHILLI
or WHAT'S HOT AND WHAT'S NOT...

This spicy little directory covers all the whole chillies used in this book, with a quick description of their heat profile and the next best thing to use if you need/want an alternative.

Prik num

Mild-medium jade green Thai chilli.

Alternatives: Anaheim, Hungarian wax, jalapeño, any mild to medium green chilli.

Poblano

Fleshy, green, mild.

Alternatives: Anaheim.

Rocoto

Fat, hot, glossy and fleshy with black seeds. Heat can vary tremendously.

Alternatives: Red jalapeño, serrano.

Scotch Bonnet

Sassy and fiery member of the habanero family.

Alternatives: Habanero, double serrano or bird's eye at a pinch.

Thai long dried chilli

Dried version of Thai long red chilli. Medium to hot.

Alternatives: Indian long dried chilli.

Hari Mirch or Indian Green Finger Chilli

Medium-hot finger of green.

Alternatives: Serrano, Thai long chilli.

Tien-Tsin/Sichuan chilli

Hot red chilli, usually found dried.

Alternatives: Chiles de árbol, long dried Thai chillies.

Red pepper

Sweet, no heat to speak of but should be fragrant.

Alternatives: Green pepper, orange pepper.

Ciliegia piccante

Round cheery chilli often referred to as a Cherry Pepper. Hot and fruity.

Alternatives: Mild chilli powder.

Morita

Slow smoked red jalapenos. Dried.

Alternatives: Chipotle.

Aji cachucha

Small, sweet and mild members of habanero family.

Alternatives: Green or red pepper, mixed with a little jalapeño too.

Fresno

Green or red. Medium. Can vary.

Alternatives: Red or green jalapeño.

Anaheim

Very similar to poblano.

Alternatives: poblano.

Trinity

A habanero varietal. Medium-hot.

Alternatives: Habanero (use just ½ a habanero in place of one trinity)

Pasilla

Dried chilli, medium hot.

Alternatives: Ancho, mulato.

Thai bird's eye

Small, cheeky and very hot.

Alternatives: African bird's eye, serrano (but double the amount).

Ancho

Mild, dried Mexican chilli.

Alternatives: Pasilla.

Guajillo

Dried mirasol chilli, fairly mild.

Alternatives: Cascabel.

Chiles de árbol

Hot, dried Mexican chilli. Slightly peppery.

Alternatives: Dried Thai, dried cayenne.

Thai long green chilli

Slightly herby, medium to hot.

Aiternatives: Serrano, jalapeño.

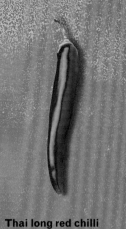

Thai orange chilli

Hot and lightly fruited.

Alternatives: Serrano, long Thai chilli.

Thai long red chilli

Fruitier than their green comrades. Medium to hot.

Alternatives: Serrano, fresno, red jalapeño

Adorno/peperoncino

Bright, spicy, HOT fresh Italian chillies.

Alternatives: Etna, Ciliegia Piccante.

Serenade

Mild to medium and commonly found in mixed bags at supermarkets.

Alternatives: Any mild to medium chilli.

Piri-piri / African bird's eye

Piri piri is the dried African bird's eye. Otherwise fresh and hot and very similar to Thai bird's eye.

Alternatives: Thai bird's eye, fresh or dried as appropriate.

Serrano

Fiery, fleshy green or red.

Alternatives: Fresno, Thai long, jalapeño.

Padron pepper

Mild Spanish pepper.

Alternatives: Shishito pepper.

Aji amarillo

Medium hot, lemon yellow to orange.

Alternatives: Red jalapeno, serrano.

Dried peperoncino

Small dried Italian chillies. Hot.

Alternatives: Dried bird's eyes, piri piri, crumbled dried chilli flakes.

Kashmiri mirch chillies

Mild to medium, vibrant colour, mellow.

Alternatives: Deghi mirch.

Jalapeño

Green torpedos. Fruity, fleshy medium hot.

Alternatives: Serrano, Thai long, fresno

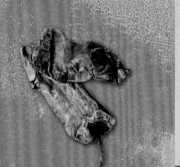

Green pepper

Slightly grassier flavour than a red pepper.

Alternatives: Orange pepper, red pepper.

Casacbel

Round, medium hot 'rattle' chilli.

Alternatives: Guajillo.

Chipotle

Dried and smoked jalapeño.

Alternatives: Pasilla.

Nora pepper

Round, russet and glossy.

Alternatives: Pasilla.

SUPPLIERS AND RESOURCES

South Devon Chilli Farm
www.southdevonchillifarm.co.uk

The Big Daddy of UK chilli farms – these chaps can supply just about anything in season. Great source for top notch jalapeños and serranos: buy in season and freeze them, or buy seeds/seedlings/plants.

Sea Spring Seeds
www.seaspringseeds.co.uk

Joy and Michael Michaud are the real deal when it comes to chilli expertise. They sell seeds and plug plants – and Joy often sends out surprise packs of interesting chillies in season! Great people, great produce.

Brindisa
www.brindisa.com

Purveyors of all things Spanish. Fantastic shop and website.

Cool Chile Company
www.coolchile.co.uk

Purveyors of all things Mexican – fresh tomatillos and poblanos in season along with the whole range of Mexican dried chillies, both whole and in powdered form, corn tortillas, Mexican chocolate, achiote paste, chipotles in adobo sauce, queso fresco and more. Excellent folk.

Chilli Pepper Pete
www.chillipepperpete.com

The original. Real chillihead stuff here. Great dried chillies, spice rubs and pastes, chilli paraphernalia and saucy gifts!

Capsicana
www.capsicana.co.uk

Good for dried chillies and excellent hot sauces.

Seasoned Pioneers
www.seasonedpioneers.co.uk

All sorts of wonderful spice blends including poudre de colombo, various curry powders and terrific chilli powders and blends. Fast delivery.

Spice Shop
www.thespiceshop.co.uk

Established over 20 years ago by Birgit Erath this is a treasure trove of herbs, spices and chillies. Portobello store worth a visit if in London.

Raan Thai
www.raanthai.co.uk

Huge Thai hypermarket in the Wirral. Great for fresh fruit and veg, and more unusual ingredients like ant eggs!

Thai Food Online
www.thai-food-online.co.uk

Amazing online retailer of Thai goods and equipment.

Spices Of India
www.spicesofindia.co.uk

Indian herbs, spices, fresh vegetables, chillies and sundry other items. Good delivery service, excellent range of produce.

Mexgrocer
www.mexgrocer.co.uk

Huge range of imported Mexican products.

Viva Peru
www.vivaperu.co.uk

Rocoto paste and aji amarillo paste available along with other Peruvian essentials.

Edible Ornamentals
www.edibleornamentals.co.uk

Great source for plants that are healthy and blooming, as well as seeds and chillies in season. All you need is a windowsill…

New Loon Moon
www.newloonmoon.com

A London Chinatown favourite, they also stock a really good range of Thai vegetables, fruits and herbs.

BIBLIOGRAPHY AND ACKNOWLEDGEMENTS

Peppers: *The Domesticated Capsicum*, Jean Andrews, University of Texas Press, 1995

The Pepper Trail: History and Recipes from Around The World, Jean Andrews, University of North Texas Press, 1999

Dokmai Garden's Guide to Fruits and Vegetables in South East Asian Markets, Eric Dannell, Anna Kiss and Martini Stöhrová, White Lotus Press, 2011

Herbs and Spices of Thailand, Hugh TW Tan, Marshall Cavendish International (Asia), 2005

Medieval Cuisine of the Islamic World, Lilia Zaouali, University of California Press, 2007

Spices, Salt and Aromatics in the English Kitchen, Elizabeth David, Penguin Books, 1970

The Food of a Younger Land, Mark Kurlansky, Riverhead Trade, 2010

Why Some Like It Hot: Food, Genes and Cultural Diversity, Gary Nabhan, Island Press, 2004

The Chilli Pepper Encyclopedia, Dave deWitt, Harper Collins, 1999

'Multiple Lines of Evidence for the Domesticated Chili Pepper, *Capsicum Annuum*, in Mexico', Kraig H. Craft, Cecil H. Brown, Gary P. Nabhan, Eike Luedeling, José de Jesús Luna Ruiz, Geo Coppens d'Eeckenbrugge, Robert J. Hijmans and Paul Gepts, PNAS 2014 111 (17) 6165-6170

Food: A History, Felipe Fernandez-Armesto, Macmillan, 2001

Africa and the Middle East, Josephine Bacon and Jenni Fleetwood, Lorenz Book, 2009

Crazy Water Pickled Lemons, Diana Henry, Mitchell Beazley, 2002

A Platter of Figs and Other Recipes, David Tanis, Artisan Division of Workman Publishing, 2008

Barrafina: A Spanish Cookbook, Nieves Barrigan Mohacho, Sam and Eddie Hart, Fig Tree, 2011

Thai Food, David Thompson, Pavillion Books, 2002

The Taste of Thailand, Vatcharin Bhumichitr, Pavillion Books, 1991

Thanks to the cracking publishing team of Ione Walder and Ben Brock.

One shot wünderkinder David Munns and team for fabulous photos and stellar eating skills.

Paul Thurlby for his amazing illustrations and Nicky Barneby for the design.

My wonderful contributors — Ricardo Zarate, Paula Briseno, Kelly Peak, Luis Inglesias, Miss Ina Williams, Liz Brooks, Khun Thip at Chao Lay Seafood and of course FRED!

All those who have inspired some of these recipes — the Kellys of Texas, Yinka, Laan Took Dee, Genet Agonafer, A.J., Omar, Malee and Anchalee at Puong Thong, and Joy and Michael Michaud.

My wonderful suppliers — lovely meat from Chris, Gary and the team at Parson's Nose, Dodie and Kelly at The Cool Chile Company, Oscar and Luis at MexTrade, Joy and Michael at Sea Spring Seeds, Donna and Geoff at Chang Beer, New Loon Moon Supermarket and Talad Thai.

My amazing friends and family, all Fred's extensive Jamaican cousins, and my wonderful mother-in-law Joyce for all her encouragement and advice. And my agents and friends Felicity Blunt and Emma Herdman.

Thank you.

INDEX

Quercus Editions Ltd
Carmelite House
50 Victoria Embankment
London
EC4Y 0DZ

First published in 2016

A catalogue record of this book is available
from the British Library

ISBN 978 1 78206 938 6

Editor: Ione Walder
Design: Nicky Barneby
Food and prop styling: Kay Plunkett-Hogge
Copy-editing: Penelope Price

Printed and bound in China

10 9 8 7 6 5 4 3 2 1